ETYMIDION

A Students' Workbook for
Vocabulary Building
from Latin and Greek

C.A.E. Luschnig

with

L.J. Luschnig

UNIVERSITY
PRESS OF
AMERICA

LANHAM • NEW YORK • LONDON

Copyright © 1985 by

University Press of America,® Inc.

4720 Boston Way
Lanham. MD 20706

3 Henrietta Street
London WC2E 8LU England

All rights reserved
Printed in the United States of America

ISBN (Perfect): 0-8191-4838-5
ISBN   (Cloth): 0-8191-4837-7

All University Press of America books are produced on acid-free
paper which exceeds the minimum standards set by the National
Historical Publications and Records Commission.

For Luke and Annie Sue

Contents

THE BEGINNINGS OF ENGLISH

English is a melting pot language. It has been shaped by political, social and intellectual factors which have taken place not only in the British Isles but also in Northern Europe and the lands bordering the Mediterranean. For over a thousand years successive waves of invasions and migrations swept over England leaving in their wake traces which can still be heard in the language we speak.

The most significant period for the formation of the English language was the time of invasion and immigration. During that time, what we now recognize as English began to evolve from a barely distinguishable group of Germanic dialects spoken by a handful of tribes in Northern Europe into the rich and worldly language we now speak.

To gain a better impression of the larger historical events which laid the groundwork for the early growth of the English language we should picture the map of ancient Europe. Some time during the later Bronze Age the geography of the continent was carved up predominantly among three large, and within themselves, loosely related groups of peoples. In the north of Europe there were the Teutons, or Germans, a relatively small grouping of land-starved tribes which were centered around the Baltic Sea. In the south around the Mediterranean the Greek and Italic nations prospered in a climate conducive to agriculture and civilization. While in the largest section of the continent, the vast heartland of Europe, Celtic tribes exerted a spreading influence which at its zenith extended from Ireland to Spain and from the northwestern coast of Europe all the way to the shores of Asia Minor.

Sometime about two thousand years ago, the peoples who then lived on the peripheries of Europe, the Germans in the north and the Italic and Greek nations in the south, began to grow in numbers and power. As this happened, they pushed towards the center of the continent looking for land and wealth. The Celts, though, were caught in the squeeze, and some migrated to the British Isles, where they displaced the earlier inhabitants called Picts. History would not leave the Celts alone, and their island refuge was invaded by the Romans from the south in the first century and by the Germans from the north in the fifth. Not surprisingly the earliest inhabitants of the British Islands, the Picts, left hardly any discernible trace on the language. But also neither did the Celtic languages contribute very much to the shaping of English vocabulary or grammar.

It was the meeting of the Germanic peoples and the Romans which shaped our language. This meeting of the two cultures began on the Continent where the first contact was made by Roman merchants, traveling salesmen, seeking new markets and sources of raw materials. And only later did armies and colonists venture into the territories of Northern Europe. The new customers for

1

Roman luxury items took along with the merchandise itself their Latin names to describe them, such as *pot* and *pan*, *wine* and *butter*. Even the Latin names for the traveling merchants who peddled the merchandise also entered the language at that early time. These early borrowings survive today in the word, *monger*, as in *iron-monger* and *war-monger* which comes from the Latin *mango* meaning a dealer. Also, from the Latin word for a huckster or small time dealer in odds and ends, *caupo*, we have derived the unflattering word, *cheap*, which describes his wares.

The Germanic invasion of the British Isles did not begin until the latter part of the third century A.D. when Roman military and political power began to wane in Northern Europe. In the beginning the Germans carried out sporadic pirating raids along the coast. But over time these raids became more frequent and the raiders, instead of leaving with their booty, began in greater and greater numbers to stay as settlers. And gradually they became the predominant population of the island. According to the traditional history of the time, the two major tribes of Germans which settled in Britain were the Angles and the Saxons. It is from the Angles that the names *England* and *English* are derived.

Anglo-Saxon England

Even after the Romans had left England for good, taking their government and soldiers with them, Roman influence remained on the island, most notably in the form of a new religion which was spreading from Rome and the Mediterranean throughout all of Europe. The Anglo-Saxons of England were converted to Christianity by missionaries sent from Rome in the early sixth century with instructions to use gentle persuasion. On account of the policy of gentle and gradual persuasion many elements of the old, pagan religion of the people were allowed to remain alongside Christianity. For this reason, the days of the week in English [except *Saturday*] retain the names of the old German gods, and the two major holidays, Christmas and the Resurrection, are named after pagan English feasts, *Yuletide* and *Easter*.

The language of learning in early Christian England became the Latin of the new religion, and the places of learning, the school and college, were the monastery and church. Through these church schools elements of Latin vocabulary began to trickle into the Anglo-Saxon language. The high point of this phase of Anglo-Saxon culture came in the late seventh and early eighth centuries.

But this was soon ended with the renewal of the migratory movement which brought the Angles and the Saxons to Britain nearly five hundred years earlier. This time the most northerly of the Germanic tribes, the Scandinavians were on the move. They were called Vikings and Norsemen. And like their predecessors, they began by raiding the coastal areas and then settled. For a brief period they ruled England, leaving as their major, but not their only contribution to our language the word, *law*.

The Anglo-Saxons quickly, though, wrested back control of the island, and under the rule of King Alfred the Great they enjoyed a renaissance of learning and political power. Alfred took a particular interest in the revival of education. But, because he had never received a formal education himself and, therefore, did not know Latin well, he encouraged the use of English as the language of the schools. This had an unexpected effect upon the English language. Until this time Latin had been the language of learning and English the language of everyday, common business. As long as this was the case, few Latin words crossed over into English, but when English started to become the language of the schools it became necessary to introduce new Latin words into English. And what had previously been a trickle gradually became a torrent of new words.

During this time something unique in the annals of European cultural history was occurring in England. For not only was the native language being used in the schools as a medium of instruction, but learned men also were beginning to write books in their every day language, English, while everywhere else in Europe at this time books were still being written in Latin, which by this time had ceased to be anyone's mother tongue. The English which was spoken and written during this time was considerably different from the language we are used to. As an example of the English used in Alfred's time we shall quote a verse from the Bible as translated around the year 1000 A.D.:

Sodhlice ealle menn spraecon dha ane spraece.
Genesis 11.1

This is called Old English and it may seem to be a foreign tongue rather than the grandfather of our language. But we shall see how in the course of the following centuries, it developed into our language.

The Normans in England and Middle English

Though 1066 A.D. is commonly taken as the year in which Norman French influence began to be exerted in England, the ground for this influence had been laid many decades earlier. As the English were not natives of the British Isles, but Germans, neither were the Normans natives of France. Their name, in fact, tells us that they were Northmen or Scandinavians. They had invaded Western France about the year 900 A.D. and settled. But unlike the Anglo-Saxons who retained their native German language when they settled in Britain, the Normans quickly adopted the Romance, Vulgar Latin of France. In the century preceding the Norman invasion of England, these two peoples on either side of the English Channel maintained an on again, off again military and political relationship, as well as a trading partnership. Ties between them were further strengthened by marriages contracted between members of the two ruling houses.

When the accession to the English throne fell into dispute in 1066, William Duke of Normandy, claiming that he had the right to rule England because he was a cousin of the last undisputed king of England, invaded the island and conquered it. Ever since he has been known as William the Conqueror.

When the Normans invaded England, they were met by a culture far more advanced than their own. Literacy and education were relatively common in England in comparison to Normandy. However, the pen, in an open fight, is not mightier than the sword, and the literate English were thoroughly conquered by the mostly illiterate Normans. For a time, it seems that even the English language would be vanquished by the conquering Norman French. For the ruling classes of English society at any rate came to speak French almost exclusively. An English writer some two hundred years later, commenting on those times, wrote that well-born children then were taught "to leave their own Language" for French from the time they were "rocked in their cradle".

But what was true of the aristocracy, who feared the politically dominant Normans and feared perhaps more that they might seem ignorant if they could not speak French, was not true of the majority of Englishmen who continued to speak their native Anglo-Saxon English throughout this period. English, however, could not resist the influence of the conquerors' language. And gradually not only bilingual Englishmen who spoke both French and Anglo-Saxon, but also the lower classes who spoke only their native tongue began to assimilate a growing number of French words into their everyday speech. Even though the vocabulary and the grammar of Anglo-Saxon changed substantially during this period, English still managed to maintain a distinct identity. And many Englishmen began to view their native language with nationalistic pride.

In 1295 the Anglo-Norman king of England found himself at war with the king of France. He was, however, unable to muster much enthusiasm for this particular war among his English subjects until he made the claim that his French adversary had threatened to utterly wipe out the English language in the event of a French victory. This appeal to linguistic nationalism swung the vote and the English fought. In less than two generations after this, a law was passed decreeing that English and not French would be the official language of England, since French had become "much unknown in the realm".

The English which was spoken and written during this period has come to be called Middle English. Unlike Old English it is easily recognized, if not totally understood, as our language. Using the same Bible verse which illustrated Old English in the previous section, we will quote from the Wyclif translation of 1395.

Forsoothe the lond was of a langage, and of the same speche.
Genesis 11.1

Modern English

With the fifteenth century begins a remarkable development in the English language. It is the time of the Great Vowel Shift, when all our long vowels begin to be pronounced with the tongue higher in the mouth, a change which differentiates the sound of Modern English from that of Middle English. Our language is difficult to spell correctly now because when the pronunciation of the words changed their spelling remained

4

unchanged, so that today several different vowel sounds are represented by a single letter. The most important cause for the retention of the obsolete spelling system (or non-system) in English was the introduction of the printing press which occurred unfortunately around the same time as the Great Vowel Shift. With it literacy became more widespread as books proliferated. And little by little spelling became standardized, but not rationalized.

During the English Renaissance (the sixteenth and first half of the seventeenth centuries) the growth of English vocabulary was enormous. Words were taken in right and left from Latin and Greek. There was, in fact, on the part of many writers of the time a conscious effort to enlarge the vocabulary of English and to make of their native tongue a means of communication to rival Latin.

The sample passage from the Bible which we have been tracing from Old and Middle English again can illustrate the development of Modern English. The verse from Genesis 11 as translated in the King James Bible of 1611 appears perfectly modern except for the anomalous spelling of the last word.

And the whole earth was of one language, and of one speach.

The size of its vocabulary is one of the most conspicuous aspects of English. It has given English the capability of expressing extremely subtle shades of meaning and has made our language one of the most remarkable inventions of mankind. And even today the growth of our vocabulary goes on apace. Technical terms are invented daily, mostly from Latin and Greek.

Exercises

In the exercises that follow, each student should be responsible for only two or three words in each group; part of class time can be spent discussing interesting etymologies.

Exercises 1: History in Words

A. *From the beginnings*: The earliest loan-words that came into our language entered through contact with the Roman legions in Germany. After the Anglo-Saxons arrived in England the main source of Latin words was the Vulgar [or popular] Latin of the Romano-Britons of the towns [or *castra*]. The words in the list below are among the earliest borrowings from Latin. Go over the list and think about what kind of words were borrowed at this early date. Notice that many are for everyday things [articles of civilization] and containers for them.

1.   Choose any two and answer the following questions [using the *Oxford English Dictionary* for the most thorough history of your words]
    a.   What does the word mean [be brief]?
    b.   What is the original Latin word and what does it mean?
    c.   What is the earliest spelling in English?
    d.   What is the date of the earliest citation in English?
    e.   Are their any significant changes in spelling, meaning?
    f.   Can you think of any other related words in English which more closely adhere to the Latin or Greek original?

2.   Choose one of the words that refers to a concrete object and write a story about the reception of the new article by our rough, illiterate and uncouth linguistic ancestors.

1. street	11. port	21. bin	31. pepper
2. mile	12. mat	22. pan	32. wine
3. camp	13. purple	23. kitchen	33. ass
4. cheap	14. pillow	24. kiln	34. anchor
5. monger	15. sack	25. line	35. fever
6. pound	16. sock	26. pin	36. mortar
7. toll	17. candle	27. tile	37. pot
8. post	18. pipe	28. wall	38. fork
9. chalk	19. butter	29. belt	39. cat
10. copper	20. cheese	30. trout	40. box

B. *The Anglo-Saxons in England: Religion and Literature*

1.   In 597 the conversion of the Anglo-Saxons began on a large scale. At this time the spread of scholarship brought many new words to our language from the classical tongues. Go over the list below and choose any two to look up. Answer these questions

    a.   When did the word enter our language [if possible also tell where it came in]?
    b.   What was its earliest spelling in English?
    c.   What was the original word in Latin or Greek?

d. Has it changed significantly in meaning?
e. Are there related words in English [from Latin / Greek]?
f. Does the word come from a specific book?

1. angel	12. church	23. nun
2. alms	13. Mass	24. pope
3. cope	14. altar	25. cleric
4. deacon	15. passion	26. priest
5. monk	16. relic	27. creed
6. noon	17. paradise	28. abbot
7. apostate	18. cross	29. sabbath [<Hebr.]
8. preach	19. devil	30. minister
9. bishop	20. disciple	31. offer
10. alb	21. acolyte	32. apostle
11. dean	22. martyr	33. saint

2. Choose one of these words from literature or culture and answer the same questions about it:

1. place	11. Chester	21. calendar
2. centurion	12. soldier	22. camp
3. verse	13. title	23. cloister
4. palace	14. cohort	24. consul
5. talent	15. triumph	25. tunic
6. forum	16. senate	26. pagan
7. farce	17. tribune	27. June
8. July	18. August	28. city
9. legion	19. salary	29. censor
10. capitol	20. merchant	30. anthem

C. *Came over with the Conqueror*: Although we may think of French imports as luxury items like fine wines and cheeses and fashions, many of the words that came into English from French are concerned with things we cannot do without.

Choose one word in each group and find its origin and story.

1. The raw and the cooked. We read in *Ivanhoe* that the native Saxon word is used for the animal on the hoof when tended by a Saxon serf, but when trussed and roasted and put before the Norman overlord its named changes to the master's nationality:

swine	pork
cow	beef
sheep	mutton
deer	venison
calf	veal

Other cooking and eating terms from French include:

lentil	bacon	oyster	gravy	sugar	onion
gelatin	sauce	vinegar	oil	spice	flour
grease	batter	suet	capon	date	saffron
raisin	paste	fruit	supper	dinner	bottle
banquet	table	feast	diet	plate	grape
blanche	almond	boil	parboil	mince	fry

7

and many others more recently than the fifteenth century, e.g.

    casserole tureen   ragout   liqueur   ramekin   croquette
    cuisine   aspic   cafe   gourmet   menu   restaurant
    souffle   puree   fondant   mousse   hors d'oeurve

2. *Joie de vivre*: Many of our pleasures have French names too:

    joy   delight   ease   revel   dance   journey
    sojourn   parlour   music   tavern   chair   park
    letter   ornament tryst

3.   Back to Nature: We can live without diamonds and rubies [<
French], but without these words that have come to us via French
we cannot even go camping or go about our daily business:

    air   rock   desert   beast   cave   gravel
    river   flower   catch   cry   delay   pass
    fail   pay   sign   strive   age   manner
    perfection   discipline   circumstance
    country   city   story   cause   merit   chapter
    silence   noise   towel   cellar   lesson   fame

4.   Roots: Our nearest and dearest are named in native words:
mother, father, son, daughter, brother, sister. But most of our
other relations have some French in their names:
        the *grand* of grandmother, grandfather, grandchild
        uncle, aunt, niece, nephew, cousin

Exercise 2: Using the Dictionary

The dictionary gives more information than just meanings of
words: it helps with pronunciation, spelling, usage and origins
of words [etymology].

1. Pronunciation: English is *cacographic*, that is its system of
spelling does not efficiently match its pronunciation.   The
linguistic game *guess how to pronounce ghoti* is a demonstration:
gh as in rou*gh* or tou*gh*; o as in w*o*men; ti as in sedi*ti*on gives
us a pronunciation of _____.

    a.   Look up these words and write down the pronunciation
symbols:
    bough
    trough
    through
    enough
    thorough

    b.   How do we say
    X-mas
    Mrs.
    PED XING

c.   Pronounce these words:

salve [syn. *balm*; compare to *salvo*]
viscount
descry
malign [compare to *malignant*]
theatre [compare to *theatrical*]
satiety [compare to *satiate*]
indictment [compare to *prediction*]
island
aisle
opossum [you will probably find two possibilities; which is
     more common?]
naive
one
carte blanche
herb
gunwale
forecastle
boatswain
chitterlings
cupboard

Compare *err* and *air*.

2.   Spelling: because there are so many anomalies in English
orthography, it is not only difficult to pronounce new words that
we meet first in our reading, but spelling is a constant problem.
Try to correct these misspellings:

repelent	deferrance
omitt	lettice
antecedant	godess
ruffly	yeild
Zues	theirselves
tradgedy	hipocrit
antibellum	sence
pronounciation	existance
Illiad	neccesary
reconize	illigitimate
malitious	Euripedes
ocassion	Charles Dicken's
abbridge	Hypolitus
messanger	spageti
ocurance	spinich
reccomendation	predjusdice
decieve	prosession
speach	succede
hermeticly	preceed
disfunction	wieght
langage	foriegn
wierd	preist
Ceasar	

3. Usage

A. *Standard English*: There are words we ought to refrain from using in formal writing and speaking. A dictionary can help here too. If a word is designated *slang, non-standard, vulgarism*, it is probably best not to use in an essay or term paper, on an application, or at an interview. On the other hand informal words and expressions add color and verve to our speaking and writing in less ceremonious contexts. Overuse of words that are obsolete, archaic, or rare can make us sound prissy or pedantic. But such words too can be used to achieve certain effects [such as humorous grandiloquence or parody of the precious].

Look up some of the words in this list and see if you can distinguish among the terms *slang, informal, colloquial, nonstandard, vulgar, regional* and among *rare, archaic, obsolete*. Consider when, if ever, you would use any of the words you work on.

Under *trot* you will find a trot [a *literal translation*], the trots, to trot out.

ain't	dibs
hopefully	whodunit
gray matter	snotty
smidgen	hoity-toity
hock [syn. *pawn*]	hobnob
hubby	highfalutin
hype	input
smarmy	enthuse
trap [=mouth]	pinko
fleece [=cheat]	scuttlebutt
fleabag	geek
smart-alecky	bluenose
booboo	pig out
gross out	feisty
flophouse	smooch
goose egg [=zero]	goon
gooey	goody-goody
buzz off	tummy
deep six	mosey
heater=*pistol*; can you think of any other terms for *pistol*?	
Greek [=fraternity brother/sister]	

Add to this list any more current slang you pick up.

Obsolete or just old-fashioned?

whither, thither, hither; whence, thence, hence	
wherefore	whereupon
wight	nimiety
hereunto	grippe
gree	quacksalver
certes	goodly
distaff side	to wit
fain	fane

10

B. *Synonymy*

1. What's in a name? Few, if any, synonyms are absolutely inter-changeable and yet all of these can be used in certain circumstances as substitutes for *name*. See if you can distinguish among them.

moniker	sobriquet	title
nickname	appellation	term
cognomen	surname	alias
pseudonym	denomination	repute
epithet	designation	handle
fame	reputation	

2. In a manner of speaking:

speech	talk	jargon
argot	cant	lingo
language	pidgin	slang
dialect	patois	tongue
vernacular	colloquialism	idiom
parlance	gobbledygook	jive
locution	palaver	prattle
babble	conversation	gab
powwow	confab	rap
chat	chit chat	tête à tête
chatter	parley	jawing

Figures of Speech: Distinguish among:

- analogy
- simile
- metaphor
- metonymy
- allegory
- synecdoche
- parable
- masque

4. Etymology: the words in the following lists have interesting histories and origins; choose one or two in each group and find their histories.

A. *History in Words*

true blue	candidate
cicero [a measurement for type]	czar
bluestocking	gorilla
frank, franchise	shibboleth
carnival	elixir
caesarian section	coach
money	mugwump
attic	assassin

11

B. *Classical Culture*

calendar
lemur
capitol
fescinine
solon
croesus
mosaic, museum, calliope
lotus
harpy
nymph, satyr
pandora
thespian
mercurial
martial
jovial
venereal
junoesque
plutonian
vestal
manes
paean
fauna
hermetic
aphrodesiac
argonaut
fascist
palace, castle
arcadian
paterfamilias
forum
symposium
castle
augean
rhadamanthine
draconian
laconic, spartan
saturnalia
bacchanalian
odyssey
cupid
herculean
promethean
titanic
volcanic
phalanx
cohort
centurion
legate
consul
sophist
epicure
stoical
olympics, olympian

C. *Interesting Origins*

hoosegow
cartel
dolmen
parachute
glamour
feckless
insouciant
fairy
bagatelle
chauffer
arbor
catercornered
fetish
country
massacre
gout
decimate
canary
bugle
babushka
boondocks
giddy
jeep
easel

Add to this list as you find quaint and curious words.

D. *Words from place names*

cos [lettuce]
babel
arras
badminton
bantam
bayonet
billingsgate
blarney
bock [beer]
bologna [baloney]
cantaloupe
canter
champagne
cologne
conastoga wagon
fez
jersey
mackinaw
mews
oratorio
sherry
limosine
meander
parmesan

cilice
jeans
lesbian
magenta
currant

E. *Literary words*

celadon
babbitt
diddle
gargantuan
euphuism
malapropism
quixotic
namby-pamby
pander
philander
scrooge
pickwickian
oedipal
hector

F. *People words*

burke
baroque
bobby
filbert
Cyrillic alphabet
gerrymander
Mercator projection
America
mausoleum
mansard
martinet
quisling
melba toast
boycott
chauvinist
bowdlerize
maverick
sadism
masochism
mermerize
guillotine
simony
sandwich
spoonerism [cf. let me sew you to your sheet]
bloomers
macabre
braille
derringer
diesel
shrapnel

Trivia

1. What month was lengthened from 30 to 31 days when it was named after a Roman emperor?

2. Which is the only day of the week named for a Roman god?

3. What islands were named for large dogs once bred there?

4. What common commodity was named after the temple of Juno the adviser?

5. What color clothes did Roman candidates wear?

6. With what was the Roman speaker's stand decorated?

7. What kind of salad vegetable is named after an island in the Dodecanese?

8. What mineral is named for an island in the Mediterranean?

9. What river in Turkey has come to mean *wander*?

10. What parts of the body were named for their similarity to small rodents?

Term Projects

1. The word diary: it is a common practice to ignore new words we come across in reading or new words we hear in passing or to pretend that we understand them. Instead of doing that for one month this term keep a list of new words. Write down the sentence or phrase each one occurred in, look it up and give its meaning and origin. At the end of the month turn in the list: be sure to collect at least twenty-five words.

2. The College catalogue: the ideal class in word origins has students from many different disciplines. Make a list of the twenty most important words in your field, explain each [with illustrations if they would be helpful], tell why it is important and give its origin and list related words. Pick words that every educated person should know.

Words in Context

She looked upon her position as one of unprecedented difficulty, only to be paralleled perhaps by that of the daughter of Horatius who figures in that interesting old *romance* which we obligingly call the Roman history.
                                        Emily Eden

Scraps of adventitious mineral that, after whole *odysseys* of adventure, have come to rest within the shelter of a glass case.
                                        Edinborough Review, 1899

A young Aurora of the air,
The *nympholepsy* of some fond despair.
                                        Byron

This youth was such a *Mercuriall*, as the like hath seldome beene knowne.
                                        Bacon

I here repeat the precise state of the question, which is very apt to be lost amidst the *meanderings* of a Platonic dialogue.
                                        Grote

The whistle sounds and the *calliope* shrieks out "Dixie" incessantly.
                                        Russell

Peopling some *Arcadian* solitude with human angels...
                                        Southey

To cleanse the *augean* bosom of the world by turning through it a river of pure enthusiasm.
                                        Alger

The inevitable English family, *paterfamilias*, *materfamilias*, and many daughters.
                                        Mrs. Riddell

Chapter One: Words from Latin Nouns and Adjectives

A.   General remarks on forms of Latin nouns and adjectives;
declension; plural

Nouns and *adjectives* in Latin are recognizable because they show
case declension, that is they change their form to indicate
different relationships in a sentence: one form for subject,
another for direct object, another for indirect object, another
for possessor, and so forth.   There are several patterns [five
for nouns, three for adjectives] of such changes in form.   These
patterns are called declensions and are designated by the ordinal
numerals first through fifth.   Only a nodding acquaintance with
these patterns [also called *paradigms*] is needed for word
formation.   It is important to learn the plurals of the various
declensions because sometimes [though not always] the Latin
plural is the only correct form of the plural in English.

> First Declension
>> Nouns ending in —a, plural in —ae
>>> alumna [*foster daughter*], pl. alumnae
>>> Most nouns of the first declension are feminine.
>>> The *base* of a first declension noun is found by
>>> removing —a from the given [or *nominative*] form.

Base: *the part of a word that remains constant though the
endings change.   The <u>base</u> is used for most English derivatives.*

> Second Declension
>> Nouns ending in —us, plural in —i
>>> alumnus [*foster son*], pl. alumni
>>> Most nouns in —us are masculine.
>>> The base is found by removing —us from the nominative.
>>> There are some other types which will be treated later.

>> Nouns ending in —um, plural in —a
>>> datum [*thing given*], pl. data
>>> All these nouns are neuter.
>>> The base is found by removing —um from the nominative.

> Third Declension
>> Nouns of this type vary widely in the nominative [or
>> subject form] and usually a second form, showing
>> the base must be learned.
>> appendix, base *appendic—*, plural appendices
>> onus [*burden*], base *oner—*, plural onera

>> Plurals: a) masculine and feminine, **base + —es**
>> index [*forefinger, pointer*], base *indic—*, pl. indices
>> b) neuter, **base + —a**
>> genus [*kind, birth*], base *gener—*, pl. genera

>> In the vocabularies, the bases and where useful the
>> genders of these nouns will be given.

Fourth Declension
Nouns end in -us [the few neuters in -u]; the plural is
spelled the same as the singular [the neuters in -ua],
but the Latin plurals of these are not used in English.
The base is found by removing -s or -us.
gradus [*step*] > gradual, grade
sensus [*feeling*] > sensual, sense

Fifth Declension
Nouns in -es, plural same as singular
species [*appearance > kind*], pl. species
series [*row*], pl. series
The base is found by removing -es.

Every noun has *gender*, but this need only be a concern in
determining the plural of third declension nouns.

Adjectives differ from nouns [in Latin] in that they change
gender according to the gender of the noun which they qualify.
Otherwise, in form they are like nouns for the most part. The
largest class of adjectives shows -us [masculine], -a [feminine],
-um [neuter] in the nominative singular and belongs to the first
[for feminine] and second [for masculine and neuter] declensions.

altus, alta, altum [*high, deep*]
The base is found by removing -us/-a/-um.

A few nouns of the second declension and masculine adjectives in
-er require the listing of a second form to show the base because
in some the -er is retained, bur in others the -e- is dropped.

ager [*field*], base agr- [cf. agriculture, agrarian]
pulcher [*beautiful, handsome*], base pulchr-
[cf. pulchritude, pulchritudinous]
puer [*boy*], base puer- [cf. puerile]
liber [*free*], base liber- [cf. liberal, liberty]

It is important to learn the base because it is from this that
compound words are formed.

There are also several types of adjectives belonging to the third
declension [and a few that belong to the third and first
declensions]. For these the base will be listed separately.

acer [*sharp, keen*], base acr- [cf. acrid, acrimony]
potens [*powerful, being able*], base potent- [cf.
potential, potentate]

Practice exercise 1

A.   Form the plurals of:

[Note that those in -us belong to the second declension]

    1.   focus [hearth]
    2.   terra incognita [unknown land]
    3.   apex [peak] 3rd decl., masc., base apic-
    4.   dictum [thing said]
    5.   corpus [body] 3rd decl., neut., base corpor-
    6.   antenna [yardarm]
    7.   medium [middle thing]
    8.   forum [public place, market]
    9.   locus [place]
    10. opus [work] 3rd decl., neut., base oper-

B.   Form the singular of [review examples]

    1.   genera [races, kinds]
    2.   data [things given]
    3.   alumni [foster sons]
    4.   alumnae [foster daughters]
    5.   species [appearances, kinds]

The words in the exercises are used in English in a form
identical with the Latin form.   Notice that for some words
alternate forms exist in the plural, using the English -s or -es
plural.   For these, either plural is correct. E.g. antennas or
antennae; mediums or media: the only correct plural form of
medium in the sense of "a clairvoyant who communicates with
the world beyond" is mediums; on the other hand in the sense of
"means of communication" the plural media is much more common.
Notice that media should not be used as a singular noun.

Optional Exercise: give the plural of

    1.   syllabus [list]
    2.   series [row, succession]
    3.   bacterium [little rod]
    4.   viscus [body organ], neuter, base viscer-
    5.   bacillus [little rod/stick]
    6.   nimbus [rain cloud]
    7.   aura [breeze, breath]
    8.   ala [wing]
    9.   carpus [wrist]
    10. cerebellum [little brain]
    11. uvula [small grape]
    12. vertex [highest point], masc., base, vertic-
    13. vertebra [something to turn on > joint]
    14. vertigo [a whirling], fem., base vertigin-
    15. octopus [eight-footed], masc., base octopod-

B. Rules for deriving English words from Latin nouns and adjectives

There are a number of ways in which Latin nouns and adjectives come into English. It is important to recognize that the rules which follow are descriptive, that is they apply to the results, words which actually exist in English. The change in the Latin word to make it English varies according to a number of factors and we cannot always predict from the Latin word what change has taken place. If in doubt, use a dictionary to test the existence [and spelling] of words you try to discover or invent. More dramatic changes often occur if the word has been adopted through the spoken rather than the written language, and especially if the word has entered English from Latin through French.

Study these examples and learn any new words:

1. No change: many words, especially nouns and adjectives, can be found in both English and Latin dictionaries. These are called *direct entries*.

> vapor [*mist, steam*]
> murmur [*rumbling*]
> miser [adj., *wretched*]

Note that although the spelling of the English and Latin words may be the same, the meanings sometimes differ.

2. a. The base alone: the base of a Latin word may become an English word.

> fundus [*bottom, landed property*]: *fund*
> jocundus [*agreeable*]: *jocund*
> editio [*publishing*], base edition-: *edition*

b. The base with silent -e added

> effetus [*worn out by child-bearing*]: *effete*
> globus [*ball, sphere*]: *globe*

c. A c at the end of the Latin base often becomes k and double letters are sometimes reduced to single letters.

> arca [*chest*]: *ark*
> jocus [*jest*]: *joke*
> flamma [*fire, torch*]: *flame*

3. Changes in Latin endings

> -ia becomes -y calumnia [*false accusation*] > *calumny*
> -ium becomes -y augurium [*prophecy*] > *augury*
> -tas becomes -ty unitas [*oneness*] > *unity*
> -tia, -tius, -tium; cia, cius, cium become -ce, -cy
>   silentium [*stillness*] > *silence*
>   potentia [*power*] > *potency*

```
            provincia [province] > province
         -gium becomes -ge, -gy
            collegium [association in office] > college
            prodigium [portent, monster] > prodigy
         -us [adjective ending] often becomes -ous
            vacuus [empty] > vacuous
         -tudo becomes -tude
            pulchritudo [physical beauty] > pulchritude
```

Note that **ae** usually becomes English e
        praeceptum [a teaching, warning] > precept

4. Various changes: Anything can happen.

    There are also unpredictable changes. These follow no
    rules, but often result in interesting words and inter-
    esting relationships of words.

        decanus [in charge of ten] > dean, adj. decanal
        praeda [booty] > prey, adj. predatory
        aquila [eagle] > eagle, adj. aquiline
        gallica solea [Gaulish shoes] > galoshes
        angustia [narrowness] > anguish

Exercise 1:   Direct Entries.   The meaning of each Latin word is
given; give the meaning of the English word if it has changed
significantly from the meaning of the Latin word. Is the English
word the same part of speech as the Latin?   Give plural of those
marked *; give singular of those marked **.

1.   pastor [shepherd, feeder]
2.   medium * [middle, in the middle, neuter of adjective]
3.   genus * base gener- [race, kind, birth]
4.   ratio [reason]
5.   quantum [how great]
6.   onus, base oner- [burden]
7.   libido [lust]
8.   vacuum [empty, neuter of adjective]
9.   circus [ring, circle]
10. larva * [ghost, mask]
11. aqua [water]
12. atrium * [entrance hall of a Roman house]
13. acta ** [things done]
14. sanctum [holy, neuter of adjective]
15. simile [like, neuter of adjective]
16. locus * [place]
17. opus * base oper- [work]
18. algae ** [seaweeds]
19. impetus [an attack]
20. breve [short, neut. of adj.]
21. finis [the end]
22. lens [lentil]
23. farrago [mixed fodder for cattle]
24. hiatus [a gap]

25.   forum [*the marketplace*]
26.   maximum [*greatest*, neuter of adj.]
27.   rabies [*rage*]
28.   Gemini [*Twins*]
29.   nostrum [*our own*, neut. of adj.]
30.   opprobrium [*reproach*]
31.   placenta [*flat cake*]
32.   lamina [*thin plate*]
33.   minor, minus [*less*]
34.   plus [*more*]
35.   major [*greater, older*]
36.   bonus [*good*, masculine of adj.]
37.   sanctus [*holy*, masculine of adj.]
38.   arena [*sand*]
39.   species [*appearance*]
40.   album [*white*, neut. of adj.]
41.   integer [*whole, untouched*, adj.]
42.   neuter [*neither*, adj.]
43.   fulcrum [*bedpost*]
44.   index * base, indic- [*pointer*]
45.   odium [*hatred*]
46.   mores [*customs*]
47.   virago [*heroic maiden, overbearing woman*]
48.   crux [*cross*]
49.   tutor [*watcher*]
50.   doctor [*teacher*]

Exercise 2:   Simple changes.   Review list of common changes.
Give English spelling, tell whether it is a noun or adjective.
Be able to define it.

Examples:

mulcta [*a fine*] > mulct [base of Latin word], noun or verb,
      penalty
jejunus [*hungry, fasting*] > jejune [base + silent -e], adj., *not
      nourishing, insubstantial*
lilium [*a flower*] > lily [-ium > y], noun
malitia [*wickedness*] > malice [-tia > -ce], noun
mansuetudo [*gentleness*] > mansuetude [-tudo > -tude], noun
aequitas [*evenness*] > equity [ae > e; -tas > -ty], noun
lubricus [*slippery*] > lubricous [-us > -ous], adjective

   1.   raucus [*hoarse*]
   2.   libellus [*little book*]
   3.   lacus [*water basin*]
   4.   prolixus [*poured forth*]
   5.   linea [*thread*]
   6.   obtusus [*blunted*]
   7.   officium [*performance of duty*]
   8.   hospitium [*hospitality*]
   9.   cratis [*wickerwork*]
  10.   inanis [*empty, vain*]
  11.   barba [*beard*]
  12.   libertas [*freedom*]

13. gratia [*thanks*]
14. conscious [*knowing with*]
15. glans, base gland- [*acorn*]
16. clementia [*mildness*]
17. impius [*not devoted to duty*]
18. aedificium [*building*]
19. uxorius [*fond of one's wife, hen-pecked*]
20. crassus [*fat, gross, dense*]
21. lucrum [*profit*]
22. luridus [*pale, ghostly*]
23. prudentia [*act of foreseeing*]
24. dirus [*fearful*]
25. dubius [*doubtful*]

Check your answers to make sure you have used only the changes
listed in rules 2 and 3.

Exercise 3:   Unpredictable changes.   Study the examples of
unpredictable changes and then try to think of another English
word which more closely adheres to the Latin original.   In this
exercise you may add suffixes and prefixes.

Examples:
     guttur [*throat*] > goiter/guttural
     cuneus [*wedge*] > coin/cuneiform

                              Fill in English word from Latin

[febris] acuta [sharp fever] > ague
ala [wing] > aisle
balsamum [a plant] > balm
captivus [one seized] > caitiff
cancer [a crab] > canker
carnalis [of flesh] > charnel
capsa [box] > chassis
acer, acr- [sharp] > eager
focus [hearth] > curfew, foyer
imperium [power] > empire
inimicum [hostile] > enemy
ferus [wild] > fierce
genus [race, kind] > genre
ingenium [talent] > engine, gin (as in cotton gin)
hospes, hospit- [guest, host] > host
humilis [lowly, on the ground] > humble
invidia [act of looking against] > envy
locus [place] > lieu, *lieutenant*
magister [master] > master, mister, maestro
malleus [hammer] > maul
mensa [table] > mesa
nepos, nepot- [grandson, nephew] > nephew
innocens, innocent- [not harming] > ninny
horridus [causing to tremble] > ordure
pinna [feather] > panache
praeda [booty] > prey
radix, radic- [root] > radish

23

robustus [strong] > <u>rambunctious</u>
redemptio [a buying back] > <u>ransom</u>
juniperus [a type of evergreen] > <u>gin</u>

Some other words of interesting origin are: *banjo, camber, counterpane, cowl, gargoyle, country, ferret, feckless, enhance, paladin, pavilion, sluice, season, fetish.* Choose one and find its origin.

Vocabulary: Learn these words. For each give one simple or direct derivative and as many compounds as you can think of. Always learn Latin word, Latin base [if not obvious from the first form], and meaning.

Nouns		Derivatives
animus; anima	*spirit, breath*	animus, animosity, unanimity, pusillanimous, magnanimity, animal, animation
causa	*cause, reason*	
corpus, corpor-	*body*	
domus [domes-]	*, home, house*	
fatum	*the thing said, fate*	
finis	*end*	
focus	*hearth > fire*	
genus, gener-	*race, kind, birth*	
gratia	*favor, thanks*	
gratus [adj.]	*grateful, thankful*	
labor, labor-	*work*	
littera	*letter*	
locus	*place*	
modus	*manner*	
onus, oner-	*burden*	
opus, oper-	*work*	
pax, pac-	*peace*	
populus	*people*	
rota	*wheel*	
species	*sight, appearance*	
studium	*eagerness, zeal*	
terra	*earth, land*	
terminus	*end, limit*	
via	*way, road*	

Adjectives

amplus	*large, spacious*	
antiquus	*old*	
bonus / bene	*good / well*	
brevis	*short*	brief
clarus	*bright, clear*	clear
dignus	*worthy*	worthy
divus	*of a god*	diva, divine

24

```
facilis    easy
       difficilis    hard
humilis    lowly
par    equal
plenus    full                              plenum
primus    first
sanctus    holy
similis    like
vacuus    empty
verus    true
```

Review exercises

1. Match English derivative to meaning of Latin base word. Tell
what the Latin base word is.

0. impervious_a_	a. way [via]
1. exterminate___	b. body
2. rotunda___	c. the thing said
3. a la mode___	d. thanks
4. pusillanimous___	e. eagerness
5. deviate___	f. kind
6. because___	g. appearance
7. corpuscle___	h. place
8. studious___	i. end [use twice]
9. pay___	j. head
10. fatalism___	k. peace
11. specious___	l. burden
12. depopulate___	m. manner
13. lieutenant___	n. home
14. gratis___	o. the people
15. exonerate___	p. spirit
16. generic___	q. wheel
17. definitive___	r. reason
18. major-domo___	

2.   Give meaning of Latin adjective from which each of these is
derived:

```
     1.    verisimilitude [2]
     2.    claret
     3.    antiquary
     4.    indignity
     5.    sanctuary
     6.    parity
     7.    primordium
     8.    breviary
     9.    amplitude
    10.    bon mot
    11.    benediction
    12.    facility
    13.    divination
```

3.   Which word does not belong [choose a word in each group that does not share a common base with the others]:

1. aquatic   aquifer   aqueduct   aquiline
2. focus   foyer   curfew   foc's'c'le
3. fin   finial   find   definite   infinitessimal
4. ingrate   grate   gracious   gratuity   grace   gracious
5. domain   indomitable   dome   domestic   dominate   domino
        domestic   doom   dame
6. diva   dive   divine   divination   divinity
7. infradig   deign   condign   digit
8. viable   viaduct   obvious   deviate   voyage   convoy
9. humus   human   exhume   posthumous   humble   humid   humility
10. studious   stud   study   student
11. compare   pare   par   parity   umpire
12. prime   prince   primer   primordial   primary   prima facie
        primacy   primitive   primogeniture   imprimatur
13. terrain   Mediterranean   deterrent   terra firma
14. vacuum   evacuate   vacuous   vaccine
15. plenipotentiary   plenum   plane   plenty   replenish

Supplement for chapter one: Latin expressions

These are commonly used in English.   Try to figure out what they mean and how they are used.

        persona non grata [non = *not*]
        habeas [you will have] *corpus*
        bona fide [in _____ faith]
        sui generis [of its own _____]
        prima facie [at _____ face]
        corpus delicti [_____ of the crime]
        modus operandi [= M.O.: _____ of working]
        pax vobiscum [_____ be with you]
        ceteris paribus [with other things being _____]
        sanctum sanctorum [_____ of _____, plural]

Some words from Latin expressions.

        maxim from *propositio maxima* [greatest proposition]
        orotund from *ore rotundo* [with round mouth]
        parson from *persona ecclesiae* [person of the church]
        limbo from *in limbo* [on the border]
        debenture from *debentur* [they are owed]
        mob from *mobile vulgus* [the fickle crowd]
        quarto from *in quarto* [in fourths]

Add to these lists any interesting Latin expressions or mottoes you come across in your daily life.   What is your state motto; does your school, dorm, fraternity have a motto [if not invent one]?   Consult your purse or pocket for Latin sayings on money and other items.   What cigarette uses *in hoc signo vinces*; what beer claims *plus vitae*?

Check-list for lesson one: what you should know

1.   Plurals
     -a   -ae
     -us   -i
     -um   -a
     third declension: -es [masculine and feminine]
                       -a [neuter]
     -es   -es

2.   Finding **base**:   remove the ending that is peculiar   to   the
declension: I -a -- II -us/-um -- III *learn special form*   --
IV -us/-s --   V -es

3.   **Simple changes**
     a.   no change
     b.   base alone
     c.   base + **e**
     d.   -ia, -tas > -y,-ty
     e.   -ti-, -ci- > -cy, -ce; -gi- > -ge, -gy
     f.   -us > -ous
     g.   ae > e
     h.   various unpredictable changes

Fill in an example for each of the rules above.

4.   Learn Latin **vocabulary**

5.   Learn any new English words in the lesson.   It helps to use
each new word in a sentence or phrase.

Try this quiz on some of the words from chapter 1:

 1.   *quantum* a. large number   b. life-style c. open excavation
      d. amount or specified portion
 2.   *virago* a. maiden b. manly c. heroic woman d. zodiac sign
 3.   *inane* a. become used to b. empty   c. lifeless d. loving
 4.   *lucre* a. filth   b. profit   c. ill-gotten goods   d. shine
 5.   *carnal* a. meat-eating b. obscene c. spiritual d. fleshly
 6.   *invidious* a. sightless   b. offensive c. requesting help or
      participation   d. treacherous
 7.   *pusillanimous*   a. generous   b. boyish   c. mean-spirited
      d. kittenish
 8.   *specious* a. extraordinary b. deceptive c. concerning kind
      d. of caves
 9.   *jejune* a. youthful b. intercalary month   c. insubstantial
      d. happy
10.   *uxorious*   a. charging excessive interest b. seizing the
      government without the consent of the senate   c. hen-pecked
      d. extravagant

Puzzle

```
        1  2  3  4  5  6

        _  _  _  _  _  _

           _        _

     7  _  _  _  _  _  _

        _     _     _

        _     _

  8  _  _  _  _  _
```

Across

1. pursuits at the three ways
7. Roman hall
8. a greater officer

Down

2. actualities
4. heroic woman
6. Romulus' ale

Context

People may go on talking for ever of the jealousies of
pretty women; but for real genuine, hard-working envy there is
nothing like an ugly woman with a taste for admiration. Her
mortified vanity curdles into malevolence; and she *calumniates*
where she cannot rival.

Edith Eden,
The Semi-Attached Couple
published in the series, *Virago* Modern Classics

Chapter Two: Formation of Adjectives

Adjectives are used to give attributes of nouns. Most of the
adjectives in this lesson are formed from nouns; a few are built
on adjective or adverb bases. As in English and German,
adjectives in Latin can be formed by adding suffixes to nouns [or
noun bases]. In English we use the suffixes -y, -ly, -ish to
form adjectives meaning *of, belonging to, having the nature of*;
and the suffixes -ful, -some to mean *having, tending to be, full
of*. See if you can pick out a few German and Latin suffixes in
this chart.

English (noun/adj.)	German	Latin
heart	Herz	cor, cord[i]
hear*ty*	herz*lich*	cordi*alis*
world	Welt	mundus
world*ly*	welt*lich*	mund*anus*
boy	Knabe	puer, puer-
boy*ish*	knaben*haft*	puer*ilis*
law	Gesetz	lex, leg-
law*ful*	gesetz*lich*	leg*alis*
burden	Last	onus, oner-
burden*some*	last*ig*	oner*osus*

Notice that in Latin the suffix is added to the *base* of the noun.
See if you can change the Latin adjectives to their English forms
by using the rules you learned in chapter one.

Latin Adjective-Forming Suffixes

A. With meanings similar to -y, -ly, -ish: *of, having to do
with, having the nature or character of, pertaining to,
concerning*

Form in English	From Latin	Examples
-al	-*alis*	*manus, manu-* (hand): manual
-ar	-*aris*	*luna* (moon): lunar
-ary	-*arius, -aris*	
		necesse (unavoidable): necessary
-arious	-*arius*	*grex, greg-* (flock): gregarious
-il, ile	-*ilis*	*puer* (boy): puerile
-an, ane	-*anus*	*mundus* (world): mundane
		urbs, urb- (city): urban, urbane
-ine	-*inus*	*canis, can-* (dog): canine
-ic, -tic	-*icus,*	*civis, civ-* (citizen): civic
	-*ticus*	*luna* (moon): lunatic

-eous, -eal	-eus	*ignis, ign-* (fire): igneous
		arbor (tree): arboreal
-aceous	-aceus	*sebum* (tallow, suet): sebaceous
-aneous	-aneus	*miscellus* (mixed): miscellaneous
-ernal, -ern	-ernus	*hibernus* (wintry, winter): hibernal
-urnal, -urn	-urnus	*dies, di-* (day): diurnal
-nal	-nus	*mater, matr-* (mother): maternal
-ate	-atus	*deliciae* (pet, delight): delicate

Notes

-ar is a variant of -al: it is used when the letter *l* occurs in one of the last two syllables of the base word [e.g. *popul-aris, sol-aris, lun-aris*].

From Latin -arius, the masculine form, are derived *nouns* in -ary meaning *one who is concerned with, one who*: *adversus* [turned against]: adversary.

From the neuter -arium come *nouns* in -arium, -ary meaning *place of or for*: *aqua* [water]: aquarium; *avis* [bird]: aviary.

Practice exercises

A. Review vocabulary of previous lesson; divide the following into **base** and **suffix**; give meaning of each part and meaning of whole.

Example: *general*: base *gener-* [genus], <u>kind</u>
             suffix -al [-alis], <u>of,</u> <u>concerning</u>
             meaning *of [or belonging to] a kind*

1. popular
2. corporal
3. corporeal
4. special
5. finial
6. modern
7. rotary
8. antiquary
9. modal
10. breviary
11. divine
12. sanctuary
13. similar
14. terminal
15. domestic
16. generic
17. animal
18. primary
19. primal
20. terrarium
21. final
22. terraqueous

30

B. Form adjectives from:

1. fatum
2. locus
3. similis
4. causa
5. tempus, tempor— [*time*]

More Adjective-forming Suffixes

B. With meanings similar to English —ful, —some: *having, tending to be, full of*

-ose, -ous   —*osus*   *copia* [abundance]: copious
                           otium [leisure]: otiose

-lent   —*lentus*   *vis* [force]: violent
                           virus [poison]: virulent
     This suffix may appear as —ilent, —olent, —ulent

Practice exercise

Divide into parts [base, suffix]; give meaning of word.

1. onerous
2. corpulent
3. populous
4. gracious [ti > ci]
5. generous
6. specious
7. studious
8. otiose [otium, *leisure*]

What is the difference between *specious* and *special*?

Look up *fulsome* in your dictionary and use it in a sentence.

kind and kind

The native English word kind meaning *magnanimous, helpful, warm-hearted* comes from the same root as kind, *a class, type* and both are related to Latin genus which gives us, among many derivatives, generous, implying that *kindness* is natural to our *kind* and to be true to our *genus* we must be *generous*.

Vocabulary: Learn these words; learn Latin bases and meanings; fill in at least one English word using a new suffix for each.

annus [after a prefix -enn-] *year* annals, annual, perennial, A.D.
         anniversary, centennial, superannuated, sesquicentennial
aqua *water*
caput, capit- *head*
caro, carn- *flesh*
civis, civ- *citizen*
copia *abundance, supplies*
dies, di- *day*
fanum *temple*   fane, fan, fanatic, profane
funus, funer- *death, rites for the dead*
ignis, ign- *fire*
latus, later- *side*
lex, leg- *law*
manus, manu- *hand*
mare, mar- *sea*
mater, matr[i]- *mother*
miles, milet- *soldier*
mors, mort- *death*
  mortuus *dead body*
mos, mor- *custom, manner, mood*
murus *wall*
navis, nav- *ship*
necesse *unavoidable*
nervus *tendon*
nomen, nomin- *name*
nox, noct- *night*
numerus *number*
oculus *eye*
odium *hatred*
ordo, ordin- *rank, row*
os, oss- *bone*
pater, patr[i]- *father*
pes, ped- *foot*
pestis, pest[i]- *plague*
radius, radi- *rod, ray, spoke of a wheel*
radix, radic- *root*
ratio, ration- *reason, reckoning*
rex, reg- *king*
rus, rur- *the country*
saeculum *age, the times*
salus, salut- *health, safety*
sanguis, sanguin- *blood*
sol, sol- *sun*
somnus *sleep*
tempus, tempor- *time*
urbs, urb- *city*
verbum *word*
vinum *wine*
vir, vir- *man, male*
virus *poison*
vitium *fault*
vox, voc- *voice*

Exercise 1 Study vocabulary; make up words meaning:

1. fatherly
2. motherly
3. during the night
4. daily allowance for food [= ancient meaning]; place for keeping [records of] the day
5. sleepy [full of sleep]
6. full of flaws/faults
7. of/for the foot
8. many [full of numbers]
9. abundant [full of supplies]
10. affected by the moon
11. of the head
12. fleshly
13. yearly
14. of/on the side
15. of the sea
16. of soldiers
17. of ships
18. hateful
19. in ranks
20. full of plague
21. of the root
22. of rays
23. of the age/these times
24. of the voice
25. watery

Exercise 2: Take apart and give meaning of each part; give a synonym of each word:

1. onerous
2. diurnal
3. osseous
4. pestilent
5. regal
6. igneous
7. majestic [major/majus]
8. temporal
9. verbal
10. verbose
11. dial
12. manual
13. mural
14. numeral
15. terrain [-ain from -enus = -anus]
16. salutary
17. temporary
18. regal
19. ordinary
20. vinolent
21. vinose
22. sanguinary
23. pedal

24. virulent
25. urbane
26. terraqueous

Exercise 3: Distinguish in meaning

```
        aquatic         aqueous
        rural           rustic
        corporal        corporeal       corpulent
        ordinal         cardinal [cardo, cardin-, hinge]
        radial          radical
        moral           morose          morale
        mortal          moral
        urban           urbane
        civil           civic
        temporary       temporal
        funerary        funereal
        sanguine        sanguinary
        viral           virulent
        virile          viral
        virulent        vinolent
```


Which is a synonym for *secular*?

        religious   temporal   parochial   sectarian

Make up words meaning a *place for*:

        water
        earth
        bones
        dead bodies
        holy things
        planets
        herbs
        sun [light]

Which costs less, entrance *gratis* or *for a nominal fee*?

What is wrong with saying *free gratis*?

What do these words have in common, *fane, fan, fanatic, profane*?

Distinguish these: *fane, feign, fain.*

Some *word* words from Latin verbum: what do these mean? *verb, adverb, proverb, verbatim, verbal noun [cf. gerund], verbalize, verbosity, verbiage, verve* [note that *glamor* is derived from *grammar*]

34

Optional exercise: Recognizing new words

1. A unicorn looks like a horse except that it has *one* [un-,
uni-] *horn* [cornu].   Explain the meanings and parts of these
words:

    unanimous
    unilateral
    cornea
    cornucopia

2. At the equinox the length of day and *night* [nox, nocti-] are
approximately *equal* [aequus, equi-, *even*].   Explain these words:

    equivocal
    equilateral
    equanimity [-ity *condition of being/having*]
    equilibrium [libra, *balance*]
What is an adjective meaning *of or relating to the equinox*?

3. Amble comes from *ambulare* meaning *go, walk*. What do these
mean?

    somnambulism
    noctambulism
    ambulatory
    funambulist [funis, *rope*]
    ambulacrum [-acrum, *place for*]
    preamble
    ambulance [< French *hopital ambulant*, moving hospital]

4. What do these have to do with *hand*?

    manumission   manuscript
    manifest   mandate
    manure   maneuver
    legerdemain   emancipate
    amanuensis   mortmain

5. Some interesting words from the new vocabulary

    dismal probably from dies mali
    pew from pes, ped-
    sangfroid from sanguis
    rosemary from mare [+ ros, ror-, *dew*]
    ewer and *sewer* from aqua

Supplement for lesson two: Numerical Prefixes

1	[I]	unus	un-, uni-	primus [*first*]
2	[II]	duo	bi, bin-, bis-	secundus
3	[III]	tres/tria	tri-	tertius
4	[IV]	quattuor	quadri-/u-	quartus
5	[V]	quinque	quinqu-	quintus
6	[VI]	sex	sex-	sextus
7	[VII]	septem	sept[i]-	septimus
8	[VIII]	octo	octo-	octavus
9	[IX]	novem		nonus
10	[X]	decem	dec-	decimus
100	[C]	centum	cent[i]-	
1000	[M]	mille	mill[i]-	
1/2		semi		
1/2 more		sesqui		
many		multus		
all		omnis		
-fold		-plex		

How Many?

sextet	cent
trilateral	octavo
unanimous	quinquennium
quadruped	octogenarian [< octaginta, 80]
duodecimal	mile
quadruple	bilateral
biennial	biannual
biceps	bicycle
November	dean, decanal
Centigrade	quintet
quadricentennial	millennium
unicorn	quintessence
trimester	centipede
quintuplets	octave
quadrille	octet
binaural	quadriplex
decimeter	decennial
binoculars	sesquicentennial
sesquipedalian	omnipotent
omniscience	multitudinous

What English number can be seen in *twins, twilight, between?*

Find the Latin numbers
   from one to ten:

```
N O T E U Q S E S
R O U T T A U Q A
M I N O V O M U M
E D U O E C E I A
T S S E R T C N N
P S E P T O E Q T
E H E X O S D U A
S E N R N O V E M
C E N T T M I L O
```

Checklist for chapter two

1. Adjective forming suffixes from Latin

   Special uses of -ary, -arium

2. Vocabulary list

3. Any new English words in lesson

Fill in chart of suffixes: give meaning and an example

-al   *of having the nature of*   vernal, hibernal, penal, autumnal

-alia *things having to do with*   *regalia*

-an, ane

-ana   *things having to do with*   **Americana, Vergiliana, ana**

-ar

-ary [adj.]

-ary [noun]

-arious

-arium

-ate

-eous, -eal, -ean   *Mediterranean*

-ernal

-ic

-il, -ile

-ilia   *things of, things having to do with*   *juvenilia*

-ine

-lent

-nal

-ose

-ous

-tic

-urnal

Words in Context

...some *inane* and vacant smile...

Shelley

Nor yet exempt, though ruling them like slaves,
From chance and death and mutability,
The clogs of that which else might oversoar
The loftiest star of unascended heaven,
Pinnacled dim in the intense *inane*.

Shelley

This *specious* reasoning is nevertheless false.

Hobbes

A very *jejune* and unsatisfactory explanation.

Blackstone

The unity of opposites was the *crux* of ancient thinkers in the age of Plato.

Jowett

Effeminate and *Uxorious* Magistrates, govern'd...at home under a Feminine usurpation...

Milton

Where didst thou learn to be so agueish, so *pusillanimous*?

Milton

I can trace my ancestry back to a protoplasmal *primordial* atomic *globule*. Consequently, my family pride is something inconceivable. I can't help it. I was born sneering.

W. S. Gilbert

...*Antiquaries* who hold everything worth preserving simply because it has been preserved. 1762

That *opprobrium* of mankind who calls himself our protector...

Clarendon

We may not propagate religion by wars or by *sanguinary* persecutions.

Bacon

It is not surprising that tried as you have been, you should tremble at the idea of a fresh bereavement; but I assure you Dr. Ayscough is very *sanguine* about dear little Charlie.

Emily Eden

A poet could not but be gay
In such *jocund* company.

Wordsworth

Chapter Three: Noun Suffixes

Suffixes can be added to make nouns from adjectives, from other nouns, and from participles. Many of these suffixes form abstract nouns meaning *the state, quality, or condition of being _____*.

English (adj./noun)	German	Latin
friend	Freund	amicus
friend*ship*	Freund*schaft*	ami*citia*
wise	weise	sapiens, sapient-
wis*dom*	Weis*heit*	sapien*tia*
dark	finster	obscurus
dark*ness*	Finster*nis*	obscuri*tas*
healthy	gesund	sanus
healthi*ness*	Gesund*heit*	sani*tas*
even	eben	aequus
even*ness*	Eben*heit*	aequi*tas*
holy	heilig	sanctus
holi*ness*	Heilig*heit*	sancti*monium*, sancti*tas*
happy	gluckselig	beatus, felix
happi*ness*	Gluckselig*heit*	beati*tudo*, felici*tas*

The most productive noun-forming suffix in English is -ness; other very productive native suffixes are -ship, -dom, -hood.

Latin Noun-Forming Suffixes

A. With meanings, *the state of being, the quality or condition of being*

Form in English	From Latin	Examples
-ty	-tas	*qualis* (of what kind): quality
-y	-ia	*miser* (wretched): misery
-ce	-tia	*sapiens* (wise): sapience
-ice	-itia	*avarus* (greedy): avarice
-tude	-tudo	*magnus* (big): magnitude
(base in *-itudin-*)		
-mony	-monia, monium	*acer*, acr- (sharp): acrimony

B. With various meanings
    -y   -ium   augur (soothsayer): augury
    act, office, place, or condition of

    -ate   -atus   pontifex (priest): pontificate
    office of

    -ine   -ina   discipulus (pupil): discipline
    act, office, art, condition of

C.   Diminutive suffixes: these add the meaning small to nouns.
The most important diminutive suffixes are:
    -ule, -le   -ulus/a/um granum (grain): granule
                                      forma (shape): formula

    -ole   -olus/a/um gladius (sword): gladiolus
    -cule, -cle   -culus/a/um pars, part- (part): particle
                                      homo, homin- (man):homunculus
    -el,-il   -illus, ellus/a/um
                                      cerebrum (brain): cerebellum
    -leus/a/um   -leus/a/um nux, nuc- (nut): nucleus
Both English and Latin forms are in common use in technical
terminology.

Exercise 1: Review the vocabulary of previous lessons and try to
take apart and define these words:

Example: animosity: anim- mind, spirit
                     -os-   full of
                     -ity   condition of being
          condition of being full of spirit: animosity is used in
a negative sense, as is animus in English, spirit of hostility.

    1.   causality
    2.   corpulence
    3.   fatality
    4.   gratitude
    5.   magnanimity
    6.   annuity
    7.   city (from Latin civitas)
    8.   matrimony
    9.   patrimony
   10.   morality
   11.   pestilence
   12.   divinity
   13.   domesticity
   14.   generosity
   15.   radicle
   16.   corpuscle
   17.   module
   18.   capsule (capsa, box)
   19.   gladiolus (gladius, sword)
   20.   grace, gracious

Exercise 2 Form words meaning:

1. shortness
2. brightness
3. worthiness
4. office of the first
5. likeness
6. largeness
7. wordiness
8. unavoidableness
9. lawfulness
10. fatherhood
11. lowliness
12. evenness

Exercise 3 Learn these two new suffixes and take apart the words
in the list:

-ism, action, state, condition, usage, doctrine, belief in/of
-ist, one concerned with, skilled in, an adherent of

1. secularism
2. rationalist
3. militarist
4. vocalism
5. nominalism
6. legalistic
7. radicalism
8. oculist
9. specialist
10. generalist
11. finalist
12. localism

Distinguish:
1. paternity from patrimony
2. maternity from matrimony
3. faculty from facility

Vocabulary: learn these words; form a noun from each using the
new suffixes:

acer, acr-	sharp, bitter	acrimony
aevum	age	longevity
altus	high, deep	altitude
aptus	fitted to	
auris, aur-	ear	
beatus	happy, blessed	
cavus	hollow	
fatuus	silly, foolish	
forma	shape	
fortis	strong, brave	
granum	grain	
gravis	heavy, serious	

41

heres, hered-	*heir*
hostis, host-	*enemy*
humus	*the ground, soil*
humanus	*human*
jocus	*jest*
latus-a-um	*wide*
latus, later-	*side*
levis	*light (not heavy or serious)*
liber, liber-	*free*
longus	*long*
magnus	*big, great*

major, majus (majes-)	*bigger, greater*
maximus	*biggest, greatest*
malus, pejor, pessimus	*bad, worse, worst*
minor, minus (mines-)	*smaller, younger, less*
minimus	*smallest, least*

miser	*wretched, unhappy*
moles, mole-	*heap, mass*
mus, mur-	*mouse*
nux, nuc-	*nut*
pars, part-	*part*
pauci (pl. adj.)	*few*
pius	*devoted to duty*
posterus	*coming after*
proprius	*one's own*
pulcher, pulchri-	*handsome, beautiful*
qualis	*of what kind*
quantus	*how much*
sanus	*sound, healthy*
satis	*enough*
senex, sen-	*old (man)*
servus	*slave*
socius	*comrade, ally*
testis	*witness*
unus	*one*
varius	*speckled, changing*

Exercise 4: take apart and define:

1. multitudinous
2. acrimony
3. altitude
4. aptitude
5. auricle
6. beatitude
7. fatuity
8. fortitude
9. granular
10. gravity
11. hereditary
12. hostility
13. humanitarian
14. latitudinarian
15. liberality

16. malicious
17. misery
18. molecule
19. muscular
20. particularity
21. piety
22. nucleolus
23. posterity
24. pulchritudinous
25. senate
26. uniformity
27. testimonial
28. satiety
29. cavity
30. service

Distinguish in meaning between:
1. property and proprietary
2. social and societal
3. nucleus and nucleolus
4. service and servitude
5. libertinism and liberalism
6. quality and quantity

Give English spelling and meaning of:
1. *triumviratus* (*trium*, of three)
2. *auspicium* (bird-watching)
3. *pontificatus* (*pontifex*, high priest)
4. *tribunatus* (*tribunus*, tribune)
5. *senatus* (*senex*, *sen-*, old man)

Exercise 5: Form words meaning:

1. tending to/full of sharpness
2. a small shape
3. a small grain
4. human-ness
5. wideness
6. lightness
7. longness
8. largeness
9. freedom
10. wickedness
11. condition of being older
12. condition of being younger
13. wretchedness
14. concerning a small heap
15. concerning a small mouse
16. a small nut
17. a small part
18. condition of being few
19. devoted to duty
20. condition of being beautiful
21. comradeship

22. condition of being like an old man
23. state of being sound/healthy
24. state of being a slave
25. act of being a witness
26. oneness
27. oneness of mind
28. diverseness
29. of a small ear
30. condition of being concerned with shape

Exercise 6:   More diminutives:
a.   Take apart and define:
 1.   cellulose (*cella*, a storeroom; cf. cell, cellar)
 2.   cerebellum (*cerebrum*, brain; cf. cerebral, cerebrate)
 3.   clavicle (*clavis*, key; cf. enclave, clavichord)
 4.   globular (*globus*, globe)
 5.   reticle (*rete*, net)
 6.   meticulous (*metus*, fear)
 7.   scrupulosity (*scrupus*, stone)
 8.   libellous (*liber, libellus*, book, small book)
 9.   castle (*castra*, fortified camp)
10.   codicil (*codex*, tree trunk, book)

b.   Form diminutives of:
 1.   *calx, calc-*, pebble
 2.   *corona*, crown
 3.   *artus*, joint
 4.   *alveus*, hollow
 5.   *cutis*, skin
 6.   *pes, ped-*, foot
 7.   *venter, ventr-*, stomach [cf. ventriloquist]
 8.   *hamus*, hook
 9.   *minus*
10.   *majus*

Exercise 7:   Give meaning of base word and an additional   word
from each Latin base:

Example: coeval, base -ev, from *aevum*, age
         other words from base: longevity, primeval, medieval

         ineptitude, base -ept, from *aptus*, fitted to
         other words: apt, aptitude, adapt, adept, inept

In this exercise concentrate on recognizing the base;   prefixes
and suffixes will be treated later.

 1.   exacerbate
 2.   beatific
 3.   excavation
 4.   infatuation
 5.   reformation
 6.   ingrain

7. gravitational
8. inherit
9. exhumation
10. posthumous
11. jocund
12. alleviate
13. pejoration
14. majesty
15. minister
16. commiserate
17. appropriate
18. dissatisfaction
19. variegated
20. musculature
21. mayoralty
22. preposterous

Exercise 8:   which word in each group does not belong?

1. longevity   evil   coeval   medieval
2. aural   oracle   auricle   binaural
3. cavern   cavea   caveat   cavity   excavate
4. fortitude   fortify   aqua fortis   fortuitous   comfort
5. granite   granule   ingrain   grandiose   granary
6. gravity   graveyard   gravitational   grievous
7. heretic   inherit   heredity   hereditary   heir
8. latitudinarian   lateral   unilateral   bilateral
9. liberty   illiberal   libertine   library
10. magic   mayor   majuscule   majesty
11. muscle   murine   musculature   mural
12. propraetor   appropriate   proper   propriety

Lesson three: Summary and Check list

1.   Noun-forming suffixes from Latin: -ty, -y, -ice, -tude
(base, -tudin-), mony, -ate, -ine
Diminutive: -ulus/ule; -olus/ole; -culus/cule; -cle; -ellus/el,
il; -leus

Know   meanings and be able to form at least one word   using   each
suffix.   For   review   form an adjective related to each noun   in
your list of examples.   [For example: **malice**, adj. **malicious**;
multitude, adj. **multitudinous**.]

2.   Learn new vocabulary.

Review of Latin nouns and adjectives, lessons one to three

A.   From   each   of   the following form a) one simple   or   direct
entry, b) one adjective, and c) one noun.   Give meaning of Latin
word.   Be able to define each English derivative.

Example: *corpus, corpor–* [body]: a) corpus, corpse, corps
b) corporal, corporeal, corpulent
c) corpulence, corpuscle

1.   animus
2.   species
3.   gratia
4.   modus
5.   genus
6.   fatum
7.   forma
8.   heres, hered–
9.   aqua
10. primus

B.   From each of the following form one noun and one adjective.
Give meaning of the Latin word.

Example: *focus* [hearth]: noun, focus (also curfew, fuel);
adjective, focal

1.   plenus
2.   finis
3.   locus
4.   onus
5.   populus
6.   amplus
7.   rota
8.   studium
9.   terminus
10. antiquus
11. clarus
12. divus
13. facilis
14. humilis
15. par
16. sanctus
17. similis
18. annus
19. aqua
20. civis
21. dies
22. funus, funer–
23. mater, matri–
24. miles, milit–
25. mors, mort–
26. mos, mor–
27. navis

28. necesse
29. nervus
30. odium
31. ratio, ration-
32. tempus, tempor-
33. vox, voc-
34. verbum
35. vir
36. virus
37. vitium
38. acer, acr-
39. aptus
40. granum
41. gravis
42. hostis
43. humanus
44. liber, liber-
45. malus
46. miser
47. nux, nuc-
48. pius
49. sanus
50. senex, sen-
51. socius
52. servus
53. varius

C. Give meaning of each base word and define each compound:

1. laborious
2. breviary
3. dignity
4. verity
5. capital
6. carnal
7. fanatic
8. copious
9. unilateral
10. igneous
11. quality
12. satiety
13. jocular
14. manual
15. mural
16. nominal
17. nocturnal
18. numerous
19. ocular
20. ordinary
21. osseous
22. patrimony
23. pedal
24. testimony
25. pestilence

47

26. radial
27. radical
28. regal
29. secular
30. salutary
31. solar
32. somnolent
33. urbane
34. terrarium
35. altitudinal
36. vacuous
37. beatitude
38. fatuous
39. fortitude
40. latitude
41. levity
42. longitude
43. magnanimity
44. minority
45. molecular
46. muscular
47. particular
48. posterity
49. pulchritudinous
50. plenitude

D.   Identify noun or adjective base:

1.   incarnation
2.   bonbon
3.   evacuate
4.   benefit
5.   eradicate
6.   irradiate
7.   impediment
8.   coordinate
9.   consanguinity
10. somnambulism
11. suburb
12. vintner
13. infatuate
14. obliterate
15. excavate

E.   Singular and plural: tell which each is and change to the
opposite number.
Example **data** plural; the singular is *datum*

1.   media   6.   memoranda
2.   focus   7.   series
3.   genera   8.   loci
4.   formula   9.   alumnae
5.   agendum   10. species

F. Match suffixes with similar meanings

```
__tude                  a. ary (use three times)
__tic                   b. lent      c. cule
__ose                   d. el        e. al
__arium                 f. ule       g. ine
__ist                   h. ic        i. mony
__cle                   j. ane       k. ity
                        l. ice       m. ile
                        n. leus
```

G. Match with meaning of base word

```
_x_0. particular        a. sinew       n. fat
___1. musculature       b. foolish     o. country
___2. rusticate         c. heart       p. center
___3. nucleolus         d. death       q. smaller
___4. minority          e. wide        r. side
___5. pejorative        f. mouse       s. swear
___6. fatuity           g. young       t. thing said
___7. fatalism          h. voice       u. like
___8. immortal          i. obese       v. wall
___9. morality          j. strong      w. nut
__10. latitude          k. custom      x. part
__11. verisimilitude(2) l. worse       y. even
__12. equivocate(2)     m. disease     z. true
```

H. General Vocabulary: know meanings of:

```
 1.  puerile             11.  invidious
 2.  onerous             12.  incarnation
 3.  farrago             13.  secular
 4.  virago              14.  sanguine
 5.  crux                15.  amanuensis
 6.  obtuse              16.  pulchritude
 7.  mansuetude          17.  proprietary
 8.  plenipotentiary     18.  libertine
 9.  orotund             19.  coeval
10.  pusillanimous       20.  jejune
```

I. Compare the following doubles:

```
acrimony--sharpness          altitude--highness
sociology--folklore          turpitude--wickedness
odium--hatred                amicable--friendly
nuptials--wedding            felicity--happiness
sorority--sisterhood         igneous--fiery
verity--truth                jejune--hungry
sentiment--feeling           science--knowledge
sapience--wisdom             carnal--fleshy
confirm--strengthen          err--stray
supervise--oversee           desperate--hopeless
```

49

Arthur's *homonym* game

Find words that sound the same for the definitions in each line.

1. laurel, body of water, to howl, reddish brown horse, projecting window, and an Ottoman governor

2. run away (from) a pest

3. a fern, to stop, and to rupture

4. expectorated, a petty quarrel, oysters do it

5. female deer, bread in the making

6. to bend, a branch

7. discoursed, part of a wheel

8. more daring (with) a large rock

9. a four base hit, the father of poetry

10. agreeable, metamorphic rock

11. abase, grounds of a mansion

12. a narrow gorge, to make dirty

13. superlatively bad, sausage

Add five more to this list.

Contexts

"We are always doing," says he, "something for *Posterity*, but I would fain see *Posterity* doing something for us."
                              Joseph Addison

        Do not, as some ungracious pastors do,
        Show me the steep and thorny way to heaven,
        Whiles, like a puffed and reckless *libertine*,
        Himself the primrose path of dalliance treads,
        And recks not his own rede.
                              Shakespeare, *Hamlet*

Chapter Four: Latin Verbs

The Latin verb has many forms which show *person, number, tense, voice, mood.* [For more explanation see the supplement to this lesson.] Of these forms only **two** are important for the formation of English words. Only two forms, therefore, need be learned for each verb, with the occasional exception of certain −i−stem verbs for which the presence of an −i− in the stem would be ambiguous without a third form. On the other hand there are some verbs for which only one form need be learned (either because the second form does not exist or because it is not productive of English words).

The two forms to be learned are *the present infinitive* and the *the perfect passive participle* (in the neuter nominative singular). This latter form will be abbreviated ppp.

INFINITIVES		bases	PARTICIPLES	
I	**portare** (to carry)	port(a)	**portatum**	(carried)
II	**docēre** (to teach)	doc(e)	**doctum**	(taught)
III	**ducere** (to lead)	duc(e)	**ductum**	(led)
IIIi	**capere** (to take)	cap(ie)	**captum**	(taken)
IV	**sentire** (to feel)	sent(i)	**sensum**	(felt)

All the **ppp** forms end in −um. To find the **base** remove −um. All the infinitives end in a vowel +re. The **base** is found by removing the vowel and *re*. In some compounds the vowel is retained. Certain verbs of the third conjugation (III) have i as part of the stem (IIIi, above) [for these an additional form in −io will be given]. All verbs in −ire also have i as part of the stem. Verbs are divided into *conjugations* according to the vowel before re: −are, first conjugation (I); −ēre, second conjugation (II); −ere, third conjugation (III); −ire, fourth conjugation (IV). Conjugations are **patterns of changes** in the present system (that is, present, imperfect [or continuous past], future) for which the forms depend upon the stem vowel. There are a few verbs called deponents which end in −ri or −i in the present infinitive. [For example, mirari (to wonder); sequi (to follow): simply remove the vowel and −*ri* or the −*i* to find the base.]

The verbs ending in −are (almost) always have their **ppp** in −atum; some, but not all, in −ire also retain the −i− in the **ppp**. But most verbs add −tum directly to the last consonant of the base. If the present base ends in a **g** or **b** *assimilation* takes place before −tum. The **g** changes to **c** and the **b** to **p** to make them easier to pronounce before −tum.
>   agere −− actum [for *ag−tum*]
>   scribere −− scriptum [for *scrib−tum*]

A dental sound (**d**, **t**) at the end of the base usually causes a change to −sum in the **ppp**.
>   mittere −− missum
>   vidēre −− visum

There are also many irregularly formed ppps. For example:
        pellere -- pulsum
        premere -- pressum
        ferre -- latum
        emere -- emptum

Practice exercises (1):   Form the ppp [in -tum or -sum] for each
of the following present infinitives.   In this exercise all -are
verbs have -atum and all -ire verbs have -itum.   Others do   not
retain the vowel.

Example errare (go astray): ppp erratum
          ludere (play): ppp lusum (note: dental stem)

 1.   audire (hear)
 2.   clamare (shout)
 3.   vertere (turn)
 4.   tenēre (hold, keep)
 5.   facere (make, do)
 6.   cadere (fall)
 7.   caedere (cut, kill)
 8.   jacere (throw)
 9.   ire (go)
10.   dicere (say)
11.   stare (stand)
12.   rogare (ask)
13.   canere (sing)

Latin verbs come into English as verbs, nouns, adjectives in the
following ways:

1.   Base alone
          present base: *errare* > **err** (verb)
          ppp base: *auditum* (hear) > **audit** (verb, noun)

2.   Base + silent -e
          present base: *eludere* (cheat) > **elude**
          ppp base: *reversum* (turned back) > **reverse**

3.   A double consonant at the end of the Latin present base is
often reduced to a single consonant in the English word.
          impellere (push on) > **impel**
          remittere (send back) > **remit**
          incurrere (run against) > **incur**

4.   Unpredictable changes may take place [especially under French
influence].
          cantare > **chant**
          retinēre > **retain**
          decipere > **deceive**
          clamare > **claim**
          fallere > **fail**
English verbs from the present bases of *capere* (-*cipere*), *tenere*
(-*tinere*), *clamare* show respectively -ceive, -tain, -claim. But

52

suffixed derivatives will usually show the Latin base:
>   contain, continent
>   pertain, pertinent
>   receive, recipient
>   claim, clamor [but cf. *claimant*]

Practice exercises (2): give a simple English derivative of each; tell what part of speech the derivative is; describe the change; and tell whether the Latin form is present infinitive or ppp.

Example: *decipere* > deceive, a verb with irregular change influenced by French; it comes from the present base.
>   *repulsum* > repulse, a verb from the ppp base + silent -e.

1.   actum (done)
2.   parare (make ready)
3.   erodere (gnaw out)
4.   sensum (felt)
5.   pressum (squeezed)
6.   solvere (loosen)
7.   clamare (shout)
8.   recipere (take back)
9.   addictum (sentenced to)
10. tendere (stretch, aim at)
11. cedere (yield, go)
12. datum (given)
13. factum (done)
14. pulsum (pushed)

Verbs from nouns

Verbs are formed from nouns usually by adding the -are/-atum endings (i.e. first conjugation endings) to the noun base. These most often come into English with the suffix -ate (from the ppp base), meaning *to use, to cause, to make*.

>   os, or- (mouth) > *orare, oratum* (to use the mouth: pray, speak) > **orate**
>   donum (gift) > *donare* (to make a gift) > **donate**
>   alienus (belonging to another) > **alienate**

Sometimes the suffix -ite is used.
>   ignis (fire) > **ignite**

Sometimes no suffix is added in the English word:

>   vestis (clothes) > **vest**
>   salus, salut- (health) > **salute**
>   flamma (flame) > **inflame**

Practice exercises (3): Form English verbs from these Latin nouns, adjectives, adverbs:

Example: *satis* (enough) > **satiate, satisfy**

1. locus
2. alienus (belonging to another)
3. insula (island)
4. opus, oper-
5. radius
6. liber
7. nomen, nomin-
8. genus, gener-
9. populus
10. ordo, ordin-
11. rota
12. miles, milit-
13. terminus
14. tabula (table)
15. humilis
16. vitium
17. decimus (tenth)
18. fluctus (wave)
19. germen, germin- (sprout)
20. lacer (mangled)
21. stimulus (goad)
22. frustra (in vain)
23. gradus (step)
24. dominus (master < *domus*)
25. rusticus (adjective < *rus, rur-*)

Tell from what Latin noun or adjective each of these English verbs comes:

1. facilitate
2. necessitate
3. marinate
4. matriculate
5. exalt
6. adapt
7. impede
8. cerebrate
9. equivocate (equi- < *aequus*, even, equal)
10. divest

Vocabulary Learn both stems. Try to give an English word from each stem. (* shows vowel reduction, explained below)

* **agere, actum** (-ig-) *do, drive, lead*
* **cadere, casum** (-cid-, -cas-) *fall*
* **caedere, caesum** (-cid-, -cis-) *cut, kill*
* **[capio] capere, captum** (-cipi-, -cept-) *take, seize* -ceive
cedere, cessum *go, yield*
clamare, clamatum *shout* -claim

54

* claudere, clausum (-clud-, -clus-) *close* -close
* dare, datum (-dere, -dit-) *give*
ducere, ductum *lead*
errare, erratum *go astray*
* [facio] facere, factum (-fic-, -fect-) *do, make*
ferre (fer-), latum *bear, carry*
ire, itum *go*
* [jacio] jacere, jactum (-ject-) *throw*
jacēre *lie* [no ppp]
mittere, missum *send, let go*
parare, paratum *get, get ready*
pellere, pulsum *push*
premere, pressum *squeeze*
rumpere, ruptum *break, burst*
scribere, scriptum *write*
sentire, sensum *feel*
solvere, solutum *loosen*
* tenēre, tentum (-tin-, -tent-) *hold, keep* -tain
vendere, venditum *sell*
venire, ventum *come*
vertere, versum *turn*
vocare, vocatum *call, use the* vox
vorare, voratum *devour, eat*

Suffixes from verbs:

-cide *killer, killing of* (from *caedere*) > homocide, pesticide

-fer, -ferous *bearer, bearing* (from *ferre*) > conifer, aquifer;
    coniferous

-vore, -vorous *eater, eating* (from *vorare*) > herbivore,
omnivorous

Exercise 1 Using new vocabulary, fill in the blanks

    1. to *accede* is to _____ to. [ac- < ad to]
    2. an *agent* is one who (-ent) _____.
    3. to *exclaim* is to _____ out. [ex out]
    4. to *seduce* is to _____ aside [se apart, aside]
    5. *transfer,* _____ across [trans across]
    6. *prepare,* _____ ahead [pre before]
    7. *permit,* _____ through [per through, thoroughly]
    8. *dissolve,* _____ [dis- in different directions]
    9. *errata* are things that have _____.
    10. *suppress,* _____ under [sus < sub]
    11. *transcribe* _____ _____ [trans, see #5]
    12. *insensate,* not _____ [in-2, not]
    13. *vend,* _____
    14. *revert,* _____ back [re again, back]
    15. *evoke,* _____ _____ [e = ex, see #3]
    16. *irrupt,* _____ in, into [in-1, in, into]

17. *convene*, _____ together [co, con, com with, together]
18. *contain*, _____ _____
19. *expel*, _____ _____ [#3]
20. *reject* _____ _____ [#14]
21. *transitory*, tending to _____ _____ [#5]
22. *data* are things _____.
23. *accident*, something that _____ _____ someone [#1]
24. *incision*, the result of _____ _____ [in-1, #16]
25. *deception*, the act of _____ _____ [de-down, badly]
26. *confection*, the result of _____ _____ [#17]
27. *occlude* _____ _____ [oc < ob against, thoroughly]

Notice changes in the stem vowel in 23-27. Can you figure out which verbs these are from. For further explanation see below.

Vowel Reduction

It is common when a prefix is added that certain vowels change to a reduced or weakened form.
When a *prefix* is added:

1. an a or e before a single consonant become i
    tenant: *continent*
    cadence: *incidence*
2. an a before two consonants becomes e
    fact: *infect*
3. ae becomes i
    caesura: *incise*
4. au becomes u
    clause: *reclusive*

Examples from the previous exercise:

    accident: base -cid- from cadere
    incision: base -cis- from caesum, ppp of caedere
    deception: base -cept- from captum, ppp of capere
    confection: base -fect- from factum, ppp of facere
    occlude: base -clud- from claudere

A few commmom prefixes are used in the previous exercise. Review these for the next exercises. They will be treated in more detail in the next lesson.

ad-, ac-	*to*
con-, com-, co-	*with, together*
de-	*down*
ex-, e-	*out*
in-, ir- [1]	*in, into*
in-, ir- [2]	*not, un-*
per-	*through*
re-	*back, again*
se-	*apart, aside*
sub-, sup-	*under*
trans-	*across*

Vowel reduction takes place in compound nouns too.

castus,-a,um pure, chaste: in+castus > incestus > incest
ars, art- skill: in+art- > inert
annus year: through the year > **perennial**
aptus fitted: not fit > **inept**

Exercise 2

The verbs in this lesson showing **vowel reduction** are
agere, actum
cadere, casum
caedere, caesum
capere, captum
claudere, clausum
dare, datum
facere, factum
jacere, jactum
tenēre, tentum

A. Explain the vowel changes, identify base verb, define prefix

Example: *intransigent*: -ig- reduced verb base of *agere*
prefixes: in, not; trans, across [-ent = -ing]

1.   pertinent [-ent = -ing]
2.   addition [-ion = act, result of]
3.   receptacle [-cle = thing for]
4.   dejected
5.   exclusive [-ive = tending to]
6.   incipient
7.   perfect
8.   conclude
9.   efficient [ef- < ex before an f]
10. seclusion
11. recidivism
12. trajectory [tra = trans]

B. Change to the correct spellings

1.   exagency
2.   infaction
3.   inclausive
4.   adjactive
5.   occadent
6.   excaesion
7.   percaption
8.   addational
9.   incontenent
10. interjaction

Exercise 3 Verb Review

A. Match with meaning of the base verb

1.	devour	a.	take
2.	appertain	b.	write
3.	dissolute	c.	push
4.	rescript	d.	do, make
5.	transition	e.	eat
6.	perfect	f.	fall
7.	dispel	g.	go
8.	reclaim	h.	hold
9.	atavicide	i.	yield, go
10.	process	j.	shout
11.	occasional	k.	kill, cut
12.	incipient	l.	loosen

B. Match with derivative from the other base of the same verb; tell meaning of the Latin verb

1.	agile	a.	admittance
2.	conduct	b.	compel
3.	crucifer	c.	scripture
4.	ambient	d.	convenient
5.	mission	e.	reduce
6.	impulse	f.	vertical
7.	imprimatur	g.	oblation
8.	scribal	h.	transitive
9.	sensual	i.	sentimental
10.	aversion	j.	actor
11.	evoke	k.	pressure
12.	eventual	l.	avocation

Optional Exercise

Tell what each is bearing:
    crucifer, aquifer, baccifer, conifer, vociferous professors, carboniferous deposits.

What does each kill:
    fratricide, herbicide, pesticide, genocide, homocide, matricide, sororicide, patricide, parricide, deicide, regicide, tyrannicide, insecticide, fungicide, infanticide, vermicide

What does each eat:
    carnivore, omnivore, herbivore, avivore, apivore, insectivore
    Add five more -vores.

Lesson Four: Check list

1.   The two **bases** of the Latin verb from
        a.   present infinitive [ends in -re, some in -ri, -i]
        b.   the ppp (perfect passive participle) [ends in -um]

2.   Know how to recognize the four conjugations by stem vowel in
form a [the present infinitive]
                I   -are
                II   -ēre
                III   -ere
                IV   -ire

3.   How to form the ppp from the present base.

4.   Ways of forming English words from Latin verbs:
                a.   base alone
                b.   base + silent -e
                c.   various irregular changes: remember especially
-ceive from *capere*; -tain from *tenēre*;   -claim from *clamare*.

5.   To make verbs from noun bases,   usually add -ate to the noun
base.

6.   Always learn both bases of new verbs.

7.   Vowel reduction takes place after a prefix:
                a, e > i before one consonant
                a > e before two (or more) consonants
                ae > i
                au > u

Anagrams: rearrange the letters to form other words

    1.   arms >>> the Roman god of war ____
    2.   salve >>> one in bondage _____
    3.   side >>> ____ *irae* [Latin for *day*]
    4.   trance >>> to eat one's words _____
    5.   were >>> a water pitcher
    6.   domus >>> _____ *operandi* [Latin for *manner*]
    7.   nous [Greek for *mind*] >>> a burden
    8.   time >>> to send out
    9.   venerate >>> tire out
    10. tide >>> a way of living > a way of eating

Supplement for chapter four: Latin and English verbs

The English verb system is a marvel of simplicity and subtlety. To appreciate this one need only compare it to the verb system of an *inflected* language like Latin. The Latin verb system is a marvel too, but of a different kind. Latin has six tenses. The tenses in English are harder to count, but there are many more than six. The Latin verb has scores of forms: it changes to show *person* [I, you, he/she/it, we, they] and *number* [I/we, she/they] and *tense* [present, various pasts, future] and *mood* [indicative, subjunctive, imperative] and *voice* [active and passive]. To express all these changes English uses very few forms, no more in fact than five [with the exception of the verb to *be* which has eight forms]. Latin changes the verb to show the changes; English changes the words that accompany the verb [pronouns, auxiliaries], but the same combinations can go with any verb and our memories are not over-taxed.

Take, for example, a regular and an irregular verb and put them through their paces.

work   do

How many different *forms* does each have?

work: *work, works, working, worked*

do: *do, does, doing, did, done*

How many uses does each of these forms have?

Work is used for
1. the *present*: I work, we work
2. the *infinitive*: [to] work
3. the *imperative*: work harder!
4. after many *modal and temporal auxiliaries*: you must work, you may, might, will, shall, should, would, can, could work, you do or don't work

Works is used for present third person singular: he, she, it works; Aspasia works, Perses works, the computer works.

Working is the present participle, used for:
1. as adjective [a *participle* is a verbal adjective]: working men and women; a working proposal
2. for *progressive* tenses [progressive tenses look at the action or activity as going on, i.e. in progress] in the active voice: I am working, we were working, she has been working, they will have been working, etc.
3. as *gerund* [a gerund is a *verbal noun* which has the same form as the participle]: by working hard we make progress; working under pressure is good for some people.

Worked is used both as *simple past* and as *past participle*:
    1. simple past: we <u>worked</u>
    2. past participle: a. active perfect tenses: we have
<u>worked</u>, they had <u>worked</u>, you will have <u>worked</u>
    b. the passive system: it is <u>worked</u>, we are being over
<u>worked</u>, this land has not been <u>worked</u> for years.
    c. as passive participle: an over <u>worked</u> expression

Do is an irregular verb [of very wide and idiomatic
application] and shows a fifth form [or fourth change]: *do,
does, doing, did, done.*   These forms are used in similar
ways to those of *work*:

Do: we <u>do</u> our homework; <u>do</u> it over.
Does: she <u>does</u> her lessons.
Doing: we were <u>doing</u> it; when <u>doing</u> well we are happy;
    <u>doing</u> good deeds is its own reward.
Did: George <u>did</u> it.
Done: we have <u>done</u> it; it was <u>done</u> before we knew it; it is
    the <u>done</u> thing.

Besides these uses as an ordinary verb, *do* has a number of
special uses:

    --in *questions*: <u>do</u> you say so? [*do* shows the tense of
        the question; <u>did</u> you say that?]

    --in *negatives*: I <u>do</u> not understand.

    --for *emphasis*: I <u>do</u> try. I <u>do</u> think you could work a
        little harder.

    --as a *pro-verb* [to stand for another verb and avoid
        repetition]: Aspasia works hard and so <u>do</u> I.

    Compare this simple and elegant verb system [*simplex
munditiis*] to that of Latin.   The Latin verb has the virtue of
being more precise and less ambiguous.   Instead of using
pronouns, the Latin verb changes its endings to show person.
Instead of piling up auxiliaries, the Latin verb has temporal
and modal suffixes to which personal endings are added.

The changes in form show *person, number, tense, voice, mood.*

    person: this part of the verb tells what the subject is.
    number tells how many [one or more than one]
    tense refers to the *time* of the action and to its *aspect* [is
        the action going on or completed?]
    voice tells the relationship of the subject to the action of
        the verb [the subject does the action of an active
        verb; in the passive the action is done to the subject]
        George *bit* his hotdog. George *was bitten* by a mad dog.
    mood tells the attitude of the speaker or writer to the

reality of the action [indicative for statements, questions; subjunctive for possibilities, purposes, hopes, fears, and the like]

For these changes, English combines its pronouns and its auxiliaries and Latin changes the endings of the verb.

For example:

person: the word for do in I *do* differs from you *do*: *facio* [I do] *facis* [you do]

number: the do of I *do* differs from that of we *do*: *facio* [I do] *facimus* [we do]

tense: I am *doing*: *facio*; I was *doing*: *faciebam*

voice: he/she/it *does*: *facit*; it is being *done*: *fit*
     he/she/it *did*: *fecit*; it was *done*: *factum est*

mood: he *does* [it]: *facit*; let him *do* [it]: *faciat*
     it is *done*: *fit*; let it be *done*: *fiat*

For the most part only the bases of Latin verbs are needed to form English derivatives and so these few examples will suffice for giving a general idea of the nature of the Latin verb. On the other hand there are some words which come from Latin with their conjugational endings intact.

  1. fiat, *a command or decree*, comes from the present subjunctive of *fio* [passive of *facio*], third person singular and means literally *let it be done*.

  2. placebo [literally, *I will please*]
  3. vide [common as the abbreviation *v.*]
  4. ignoramus
  5. caveat [cf. *caveat emptor*]
  6. recipe [cf. R̷]
  7. habitat [from the opening of descriptions of animals or plants, *it dwells*]
  8. deficit
  9. veto
10. imprimatur
11. floruit
12. tenet
13. memento
14. caret [^], *there is lacking*
15. mandamus
16. habeas corpus
17. exit [cf. *exeunt omnes*]

Chapter Five: Prefixes from Latin

The most common Latin prefixes are derived from *prepositions*.   They are added most frequently to **verb bases**, but also to noun and adjective bases.

English has native prefixes of a similar kind, but these are no longer as productive as those from Latin.

Native word	Compare to Derivative from Latin
onrush	incursion
uphold	sustain
overturn	subvert
withstanding	constant
bygone	preterite
backslide	relapse
outcome	event
foreknowledge	prescience
afterword	postscript
underwrite	subscribe

There are also prefixes which are not derived from prepositions.

English un- corresponds to Latin *in-* [2]:
    unfeeling   insentient

English *all*, as prefix all-, al- corresponds to Latin *omni-*:

    almighty   omnipotent
    all-knowing   omniscient

Before studying the prefixes the student should have clearly in mind two linguistic phenomena.
    1. Vowel weakening [see lesson 4]
    2. Assimilation [base, *simil-*, *like*] is *the act of making one thing like [to = ad-] another.*   Sometimes a consonant at the end of a prefix changes so that it will be easier to say before the first consonant of the base word.

For example:
    ad-, *to* becomes ac- before c; **as-** before **s**
        ad-cede > accede
        ad-similation > assimilation

    com- becomes cor- before r
        com-rupt > corrupt

    After ex- an initial **s** is dropped in English
        ex-spect > expect
        ex-stirpate > extirpate

The variations will be listed with the prefixes.

Learn these prefixes from Latin. * the most productive.

* 1. a-, ab-, abs- *away from, off, badly* [The usual form is *ab*;
a- is used before m, p, v; *abs* before c, t.]
    Examples: abrupt (broken off)
         avert (turn away)
         abstract (drawn away)

* 2. ad- *to, toward, against, intensely* [ad appears also as ac-
(before c, q), af-, ag-, al-, an-, ap-, ar-, as-, at-, and a-
(before sc, sp, st, gn).]
    Examples: advent (a coming towards)
         accurate (attended to)
         annotate (add notes to)
         assent (feel to, agree)

3. ambi- *around, about, on both sides* [amb- before vowels]
    Examples: ambiguous (going around, uncertain)
         ambidextrous (right-handed on both sides)

* 4. ante- *before, in front of, ahead of*
    Example: antecede (go before)

* 5. circum- *around*
    Examples: circumcise (cut around)
         circumflex ([something] bent around)

6. cis- *on this side of*
    Examples: cisalpine (on this side of the Alps)
         cislunar (on this side of the moon)

* 7. com- *with, together* [com- before b, p, m; cor- before r;
col- before l; co- before h, gn and usually before vowels; con-
before all other consonants.]
    Examples: colloquium (a speaking together)
         corrode (gnaw thoroughly)

* 8. de- *down from, off, utterly*; this prefix may imply removal
or cessation and it may give a bad (or negative) sense to the
word.
    Examples: devolve (roll down)
         deformed (ill/badly formed)
         defoliate (remove the leaves)

* 9. dis- *apart, in different directions, at intervals*; it can
also have a negative force. [di- before voiced consonants; dif-
before f; sometimes de- under French influence: depart, defy]
    Examples: differ (bear/carry apart)
         dispel (push in different directions)

* 10. ex-, e- *out from, out of, off, away, away from, thoroughly*
[ef before f]
    Examples: event (outcome)
         extol (raise out)
         expect (look out, await)

11. extra- {variant, extro-} *outside, beyond*
     Example: extraordinary (beyond the rank)

* 12.   in-(1) *in, into, on, toward, against* [il- before l; im-
before b, m, p; ir- before r; sometimes en- under French
influence.]
     Examples: incise (cut into)
          impel (push on)

* 13.   in-(2) *not, lacking, without* [i before gn; other changes
as in-(1)]
     Examples: illegal (unlawful)
          ignoble (not noble)

* 14.   inter- *among, between, at intervals, mutually, each other*
[intel- before l]
     Examples: intercept (take between)
          intercede (come between)
          intellect (a choosing between)

15. infra- *below, beneath, inferior to, after, later*
     Example: infrared

16. intra- *in, within, inside of*
     Example: intramural (within the walls)

17. intro- *in, into, inward*
     Example: introduce (lead into)

18. juxta- *near, beside*
     Example: juxtapose (put beside)

* 19.   ob- *toward, against, across, in the way of, opposite to,
down, for, out of, intensely* [o- before m; oc- before c; of-
before f; op- before p.]
     Examples: oblong (long across)
          offer (bring for)
          obdurate (hardened against)

* 20.   per- *through, by, thoroughly, away, badly, to the bad*
[pel- before l]
     Examples: permeate (pass through)
          perfidy (bad faith)
          pellucid (thoroughly clear/bright)

* 21.   post- *behind, after*
     Examples: postpone (put after)
          postnatal (after birth)

* 22.   pre- [Latin prae-] *before, in advance, in front of,
headfirst, at the end*
     Examples: precede (go before)
          pretend (spread in front, give as an excuse)

23.   preter- [Latin praeter] *past, beyond*
        Examples: preterite (gone past)
            preternatural (beyond what is natural)
            preterpostmodernism (beyond the post-modernist period)

* 24. pro- *forth, for, forward, publicly, instead of*
[before vowels, prod-]
        Examples: proclaim (shout publicly/forth)
            proceed (go forward)

* 25. re- *back, again, against, behind* [red- before vowels]
        Examples: repel (push back)
            record (bring back to mind)
            redeem (buy back)

26.   retro- *backwards, behind*
        Example: retrogressive (tending to step/move backwards)

* 27. se- *aside, apart, away* [sed- before vowels]
        Examples: secure (away from/free from care)
            seduce (lead apart)

28.   sine- *without*
        Example: sinecure (without [the] care [of souls])

* 29.   sub- *under, inferior, secondary, less than, in place of,
secretly* [suc- before c;   suf- before f;   sug- before g;   sum-
before m;   sup- before p;   sur- before r;   sometimes sus- before c,
p, t.]
        Example: subtract (draw from under)

30.   subter- *beneath, secretly*
        Example: subterfuge (evasion, fleeing in secret)

* 31.   super- *over, above, excessively, beyond* [sur- under
French influence: surtax, surrealism, surcharge]
        Example: superimpose (put over/on top)

32.   supra- *above, over, greater than, preceding*
        Example: suprarenal (above the kidney)

* 33.   trans- *across, over, beyond, through, very* [tra-, tran-]
        Examples: transport (carry across/over)
            transgress (step across)

Exercise 1 Practice assimilating:

1. ad-similation
2. in-pel
3. sub-fer
4. ex-rupt
5. com-vert
6. trans-scribe
7. ab-cess
8. ad-claim
9. ex-fact*
10. com-tain
11. ad-capt*
12. ad-sent
13. ab-tract
14. ad-quisitive
15. com-loquy
*practice vowel reduction on these

Exercise 2 Make up words meaning (using verbs from last lesson):

1. go (yield) back
2. shout forth
3. lead into
4. bear toward/against
5. send under
6. get ready in advance
7. write under
8. feel differently
9. call out
10. turn to the bad
11. lead apart
12. come together again
13. hold/keep through
14. give to
15. push out
16. throw in between
17. close in
18. thoroughly done/made
19. close off
20. come around

Exercise 3: Take apart and define

1. transmit
2. collate
3. suppress
4. compare
5. declaim
6. proscribe
7. resent
8. resolve
9. provoke
10. diverse
11. consensus

12. secede
13. advent
14. transient
15. abstain
16. interrupt
17. abject
18. excise
19. precept
20. preclude
21. defect
22. abrupt
23. intervene
24. circumscribe
25. antecede
26. intercept
27. postscript
28. supercede
29. object
30. oppress
31. omit
32. commit
33. admit
34. remit
35. submit

Take apart and define these words which use noun bases:

1. devious
2. obvious
3. impervious
4. supernumerary
5. juxtamarine
6. circumlunar
7. extraterrestrial
8. subterranean
9. immure [murus, *wall*]
10. intravenous [vena, *vein*]

Exercise 4:   Using the new prefixes, make up 10 words from each of these verbs:

Example: venire, ventum > advent, convent, invent, convene, reconvene, convenient, inconvenience, subvention, prevent, eventual, intervene, circumvent, supervene, contravene [also, *avenue, parvenu, adventure, souvenir, provenance*]

1. ducere, ductum
2. facere, factum
3. cedere, cessum
4. tenēre, tentum
5. capere, captum

Exercise 5   Make up 5 words using each new prefix.
Example: omit, offer, occur, oblong, obvious, obdurate, object, occasion, oppress, occlusion, oppose, observe, obsequious, obtund

Vocabulary: Learn these verbs; make up derivatives for each stem

canere, cantum *sing*
cernere, cretum *sift*
condere, conditum *build, store, hide*
currere, cursum *run*
dicere, dictum *say, speak*
emere, emptum *buy, procure*
flectere, flexum *bend*
fundere, fusum *pour*
gerere, gestum *carry, wage*
haerere, haesitum [-haesum] *cling, stick*
legere, lectum *collect, gather, choose, read*
ludere, lusum *play*
pendere, pensum *hang, weigh*
petere, petitum *aim at, seek*
ponere, positum *put, place*
portare, portatum *carry*
prehendere, prehensum *seize*
quaerere, quaesitum (-quirere, -quisitum) *seek, ask*
rogare, rogatum *ask*
scandere (-scendere, -scensum) *climb*
secare, sectum *cut*
servare, servatum *save*
sistere, statum *set, stand*
stare, statum *stand*
sumere, sumptum *take (up)*
tendere, tentum/tensum *stretch, spread, aim*
trahere, tractum *draw, drag*
uti, usum *use*
vadere, -vasum *go, make one's way*
vincere, victum *conquer, win*
vivere, victum *live*

Exercise 5:   use new verbs and prefixes.   Take apart and define
each; give at least one other English word from the same Latin
verb.
   Example: survive: sur- [from super] *beyond* + vive *live*
      Other words: revive, vivacious, vivid, victuals

1.   abscond
2.   edict
3.   recondite
4.   exempt
5.   infuse
6.   append
7.   appetite
8.   composite
9.   desist
10.   contend
11.   interdict
12.   perpetual
13.   peremptory
14.   impetus
15.   compendium [-ium, *a thing*]

16. discern
17. incline
18. deflect
19. transport
20. cohere
21. apprehend
22. surrogate
23. perquisite
24. recant
25. ascend
26. convivial
27. insect
28. pervade
29. assume
30. observe
31. intersect
32. contract
33. abuse
34. evict
35. intellect
36. abrogate
37. arrogate
38. derogate
39. interrogate
40. acquire

Exercise 6: Make up words meaning:

1. speak against
2. poured forth
3. play to
4. hang under
5. seek with
6. put after
7. stand out
8. stretch before/in front
9. stand to
10. sing back
11. sifted apart
12. rouse against
13. bend down
14. stick to
15. seize together
16. sought back in advance
17. climb down with
18. of living together
19. use thoroughly
20. make one's way away/out
21. choose apart

Prefix scramble: unscramble each to spell a prefix; the underscored letters spell a word.

XUTJA   CRUMIC   RANTS   TRINE   PURES
        FIRAN   NEAT   SCI

- - - - - - - -

70

Exercise 7 Some denominatives using prefixes: take apart, define each part.

Note: -ion, *act, result of*; -ive, *tending to*

1. evacuate
2. assimilate
3. exaggerate
4. exacerbate
5. obliterate [littera, *letter*]
6. accumulate [cumulus, *heap*]
7. reiterate [iterum, *again*]
8. excoriate [corium, *hide, skin*]
9. transliterate
10. incarcerate [carcer, *prison*]
11. excavate
12. eradicate
13. irradiate
14. exonerate
15. infatuate
16. cooperate
17. incorporate
18. enunciate [nuntius, *message*]
19. investigate [vestigium, *footprint, trace*]
20. corrugate [ruga, *wrinkle*]
21. exculpate [culpa, *fault*]
22. depreciate [pretium, *price*]
23. deprecate [prex, prec-, *prayer*]
24. decapitate
25. concatenation [catena, *chain*]
26. exaltation [altus, *high*]
27. superannuated
28. adaptation
29. inaugurate [augur, *increaser, seer*]
30. abbreviate [brevis, *short*]
31. incarnation [caro, carn-, *flesh*]
32. indentation [dens, dent-, *tooth*]
33. predominate [dominus, *master* < domus]
34. inflammation [flamma, *flame*]
35. counterreformation [*counter* < contra]
36. elaborate [labor, *work*]
37. regenerate
38. degenerate
39. collaborate
40. alleviate [levis, *light*]
41. corroborate [robor, *strength*]
42. illuminate [lumen, lumin-, *light*]
43. eliminate [limen, limin-, *threshhold*]
44. alliterate
45. inoculate [oculus, *eye*]
46. annihilate [nihil, *nothing*]
47. denominative
48. innovate [novus, *new*]
49. insinuate [sinus, *wave, fold*]
50. approximate [proximus, *nearest*]
51. defoliate [folium, *leaf*]

71

Supplement for chapter five: Expressions using prefixes

ab incunabulis *from the cradle*
    What is an incunabula?

ab ovo *from the egg*
    Give three other derivatives of ovum, *egg*

ad libitum *at one's pleasure* [ad lib.]

ante bellum *before the war*
    Give two additional derivatives of bellum.

cum grano salis *with a grain of salt*
    English *salary* comes from Latin sal, *salt*; explain why.

Dominus vobiscum *The Lord be with you*
    What does *A. D.* stand for?
    What does pax vobiscum mean?

de gustibus non est disputandum *there's no arguing about tastes*
    Can you think of another word from Latin gustis?

deus ex machina *the god from the machine*

in vino veritas *in wine, truth*

mens sana in corpore sano *a sound mind in a sound body*

inter nos *among ourselves*

per diem *for each day*
    What does per annum mean?

ex post facto *from after the fact*

pro bono publico *for the public good*

sub rosa *under the rose* [i.e. in private]

sub specie aeternitatis *under the sight of eternity*

Check list for chapter five

1. Assimilation: the change in a final consonant of a prefix for ease in pronunciation before the first consonant of the base word. Make a list of all prefixes that assimilate and give one example of each change.

E. g. *a, ab, abs:* *averse, abominate, abduct, abstruse, abscess*

ad, ac, af, ag, al, an, ap, ar, as, at, a: *adversary, acquire, accumulate, affirm, aggressor, alleviate, annunciation, approve, arrive, assent, attend, ascribe*

2. Learn all prefixes. Make a list of all prefixes which can be used to mean very. Make a list of all prefixes that can be used to mean not or in any negative sense.

3. Learn both bases of all new verbs. Learn a derivative to associate with each base.

Words in Context

Women are soft, milde, pittifull, and flexible;
Thou, sterne, *obdurate*, flintie, rough, remorselesse.
                                                     Shakespeare

They have joined the most *obdurate* consonants without one *intervening* vowel.
                                                     Swift

Do not affect little shifts and *subterfuges* to avoid the force of an argument.
                                                     Watts

Many of the best institutions moulder into *sinecures*. [1800]

He shall do this or else I do *recant* the pardon that I late pronounced here.
                                                     Shakespeare

No, of course not; what with all her children, and what with making war and making peace, and giving balls and *proroguing* Parliaments, and the Government always changing, she has not much time for visiting, poor thing!
                                                     Emily Eden

The chaplain was the Reverend Cyril Starr, and all that Crabtree had encountered to date was a sphinxlike appearance and a *perturbing* smile at any reference to higher things.
                                                     Michael Campbell

Chapter Six: The Present Base of Latin Verbs

There are many suffixes added to verb bases to form nouns,
adjectives and other verbs.   Some are added to the **present base**
and others to the **ppp base.**   This lesson will treat those added
to the **present base.**   Before beginning the new material, it is
advisable to review verbs from previous lessons, paying special
attention to the present bases.

1.   Noun-forming suffixes

-or [Latin -or] *condition of being*
    r·igēre, *be stiff* > **rigor:** *condition of being stiff*

-ium, -y [Latin -ium] *act of, something connected with the*
    act of {-cium > -ce; -gium > -ge}
    colloqui, *speak together* > **colloquium, colloquy:** *the*
    act of speaking together

-ion [Latin -io, ion-] *act or result of*
    legere *collect* > **legion:** *result of gathering [troops]*

-men [Latin -men] *result or means of*
    regere *guide, control* > **regimen:** *means of controlling*

-ment [Latin -mentum] *result of means of an act*
    impedire *hinder* > **impediment:** *means of hindering*

-bulum, -ble [Latin -bulum, -bula] *means, instrument,*
    place, or thing for
    stare *stand* > **stable:** *place for standing*

-culum, -cle [Latin -culum] *means, place for, thing for*
    currere *run* > **curriculum:** *place for running*

Practice exercise A: Take apart and define parts

Example: **presentiment** <u>pre</u> *before* <u>senti</u> *feel[ing]* <u>ment</u> *means of*

1.   error
2.   vocabulary
3.   condiment
4.   comportment
5.   segment [seg- = sec-]
6.   tenement
7.   inducement
8.   discernment
9.   clamorous
10.   cement [< caed-ment]
11.   tenor
12.   compendium
13.   argument [arguere *make clear*]
14.   vehicle [vehere *convey*]

75

15. monument [monere *warn*]
16. option [optare *wish*]
17. fervor, ferment [fervere *boil*]
18. miracle [mirari *wonder at*]
19. foment [fovere *warm*]
20. experiment [experiri *try, test*]
21. emolument [emoliri *accomplish* < "to grind out": a miller's
     fee for grinding grain]
22. sepulchre [< sepulcrum < sepelire *bury*]
23. ardor [ardere *burn*]
24. vigor [vigere *thrive*]
25. nutriment [nutrire *nourish*]

Vocabulary: learn these, especially those marked *

* alere, altum   *grow, nourish*
* augēre, auctum   *increase*
candere   *shine, be white*
* creare, creatum   *create*
* docēre, doctum   *teach*
fervēre   *boil*
* frangere (frag-), fractum   *break*
horrēre   *shudder, stand stiff*
liquēre   *be fluid, be clear*
* loqui, locutum   *speak*
lucēre   *shine, be light*
* rapere, raptum   *snatch*
* regere, rectum   *move in a straight line, guide, direct, rule*
solēre, solitum   *become accustomed*
* specere, spectum   *look at*
studēre   *be diligent, be eager, study*
terrēre   *frighten*
timēre   *fear*
tremere   *quake, tremble*
* valēre   *be well*

Practice exercise B: Take apart and define parts; give one
additional derivative for each verb

1.   augment
2.   candor
3.   document
4.   fragmentary
5.   humorous
6.   liquor
7.   obloquy
8.   regimen
9.   specimen
10. studious
11. terror
12. timorous
13. tremor
14. valorous
15. colloquium

76

16. fervor
17. alimentary
18. soliloquy [solus, *alone*]
19. tedium [taedere, *be weary*]
20. auspice [au < avis, *bird*]

2. Adjective-forming suffixes

A. Present participles and nouns from present participles

       -nt -*ing* [Latin -ns, -nt-]
       -nce, -ncy *state or condition of* _____*ing* [Latin -ntia]

            I portare > important *bringing in* > importance
           II tenēre > continent *holding together* > continence
          III vertere > inadvertent *not turning to* > inadvertence
         IIIi facere > efficient *making thoroughly* > efficiency
           IV sentire > sentient *feeling* > sentience

Although many of the English derivatives follow the Latin stem
vowel before -nt, others, especially those showing French
influence have -ant, regardless of the Latin stem vowel. This is
especially common if the English word is a noun.
            tenant *one holding* [< tenere]
            pendant *something hanging* [< pendere]; but cf.pendent,
                 hanging

Note: the suffix -nt as a noun means *one* ____*ing* or *something*
       ____*ing*.

B. Gerunds

       -nd, -ndum [pl. -nda] *that which must be* ____
            augend *thing to be increased*
            agendum *thing to be done, that which must be done*
            agenda *things to be done; a list of things to be done*

       -ous may be added to form adjectives from the forms in -nd
            tremendous *of something to be quaked at*

Practice exercise C: Make up words meaning:

1. not leading/driving across
2. state of not leading across
3. one ruling
4. state, condition of ruling
5. hanging down
6. state of hanging down
7. standing together
8. state of standing together
9. falling on

10. state of falling on
11. making thoroughly [out]
12. condition of making thoroughly
13. going before
14. act of going before
15. one doing/driving
16. condition of doing/driving
17. feeling
18. condition of feeling
19. loosening
20. condition of loosening
21. thing to be drawn [dragged] under
22. thing to be added
23. thing to be divided
24. thing to be reduced [minuere]
25. things to be corrected [corrigere]

Define:

1. student
2. intermittent
3. accident
4. repellent
5. incipient
6. claimant
7. docent
8. deference
9. important
10. cadence
11. experience [experiri *try, test*]
12. valiant
13. inference
14. attendance
15. tendency
16. incontinence
17. interdependence
18. recipient
19. prevalent
20. consistent

C. Other adjective-forming suffixes added to the present base

   -id [Latin -idus] tending to
        squalid [< squalēre to be filthy] tending to be filthy

   -ile [Latin -ilis] able to be
        docile able to be taught

   -ble [Latin -bilis] able to be
        arable [< arare to plow] able to be plowed

   -acious [Latin -ax, -ac-] tending to
        audacious [< audēre dare] tending to dare

   -ulous [Latin -ulus] tending to
        credulous [<credere believe] tending to believe

   -uous [Latin -uus] tending to
        innocuous [< nocēre to harm] tending not to harm

Vocabulary

* audire, auditum hear
esse, futurum be
fari, fatum speak
fidere trust, rely on
fluere, fluxum flow
jacēre lie
* manēre, mansum remain
migrare, migratum move, change one's place of living
mordēre, morsum bite
* nasci, natum be born
oriri, ortum rise
paenitēre repent
placēre, placitum please, be agreeable
posse [pot-] be able
salire, saltum leap, jump [-silire]
scire know
sedēre, sessum sit
* sequi, secutum follow
stringere, strictum draw tight
* tangere, tactum touch [-ting-]
* vidēre, visum see

* omni- all

Exercise 1   Make up ten English words from each of the verbs
marked *.

Example: nasci, natum: nascent, renascence, Renaissance, natal,
nation, native, pre-natal, nature, agnate, adnate, innate,
cognate, naive

79

Exercise 2 Make up words meaning

1.   thing to be increased
2.   tending to be shining white
3.   able to be taught
4.   breakable
5.   tending to be moist [humēre, *to be moist*]
6.   talkative [tending to talk]
7.   tending to be seen through
8.   tending to be afraid
9.   tending to quiver
10.   tending to be strong
11.   able to be heard
12.   one not speaking
13.   trusting with
14.   flowing
15.   lying under
16.   remaining through
17.   one moving out
18.   biting
19.   being born
20   rising
21.   repenting
22.   being thoroughly [=together] pleased
23.   leaping
24.   state of knowing
25.   being able
26.   jumpimg back

Exercise 3 Take apart and define each part

1.   adjacent
2.   audience
3.   essence
4.   affable
5.   diffident
6.   confluence
7.   immanent
8.   renascence
9.   impotent
10.   nescience [ne- *not*]
11.   consequence
12.   sedentary
13.   astringent
14.   evident
15.   tangent
16.   contingent
17.   evident
18.   conspicuous
19.   continuous
20.   tenacious
21.   audacious
22.   invalid
23.   rapacity

24. loquacity
25. eloquent
26. current
27. arrogant
28. subtrahend
29. vivid
30. vivacious
31. belligerent
32. illegible
33. eligible
34. capacious
35. capacity
36. subjacent
37. efficacious
38. competent
39. subsistence
40. extant
41. consistency
42. deficient
43. convenience
44. horrendous
45. tremendous
46. infancy
47. inaudible
48. inconsequential
49. essential
50. existential

Using new words:

1. bibulous [bibere *drink*]
2. ardent [ardēre *burn*]
3. caloric [calēre *be warm*]
4. liniment [linere *smear*]
5. livid [livēre *be black and blue*]
6. rancid [rancēre *stink*]
7. stupor [stupēre *be stunned*]
8. torpid [torpēre *be numb*]
9. querulous [queri *complain*]
10. promiscuous [miscere *mix*]
11. garrulous [garrire *chatter*]

Exercise 4   Make up 10 words using each of the new suffixes

Example: -nd- [including -ndous, -ndum]

agenda	horrendous	memorandum	addendum
corrigendum	tremendous	reprimand	nuntiandum
baptizand	multiplicand	dividend	crescendo
subtrahend	minuend	stupendous	legend
referendum	gerund	viand [< vivenda]	reverend
modus operandi		modus vivendi	
innuendo	propaganda		

81

3. Verb-forming suffixes

A. Inchoatives are verbs formed from other verbs with the meaning *begin to*.

-sc- [Latin *-scere*] added to present base *begin to*
The suffix *-sc-* sometimes becomes -ish in English.

alere *grow* > coalesce *begin to grow together*
florēre *to flower* > efflorescent *beginning to flower out*
creare *form, create* > crescere *begin to be formed, increase* > crescent *beginning to increase*

B. Other verbal suffixes
-fy *to make* < -ficare < facere
-fic *making* [adjective-forming suffix]
deify *to make into a god* < deus
beatific *making blessed* < beatus

-igate *to drive, to cause to be* < agere
navigate *drive a ship*

Exercise 5: Take apart and define parts; answer any questions.

1. unify
2. clarify
3. amplify
4. dignify
5. beatify
6. modify
7. mortify
8. sanctify
9. satisfy
10. qualify
11. quantify
12. specify
13. ossify
14. gratify
15. fortify

Give one additional word using the noun/adjective base of each of the words listed above, # 1-15. Example: sanctus [# 8] > *saint, sanctity, sanctimony, sanctum sanctorum, inner sanctum, sanctuary, sacrosanct, sanctitude, corposant, sanction, Sanctus*

Make up or find ten additional words using the suffix -fy or -fic.

16. circumnavigate
17. castigate [castus *pure, chaste*; cf. incest]
18. variegate
19. fumigate
20. excrescence

21. obsolescence
22. convalesce
23. incandescence
24. coalescent
25. fluorescent

Review exercise: make up words meaning

1.   able to be used
2.   going across
3.   means of sifting in different directions
4.   placing together
5.   asking to [oneself]
6.   means of storing
7.   running back
8.   things to be done
9.   to make clear
10. taking on
11. condition of not feeling
12. concerned with climbing across
13. following under
14. knowing all
15. [thing] touching
16. condition of knowing with
17. sticking together
18. thing to be read
19. [thing] cutting
20. causing to stand [= setting] together
21. standing out
22. lively [tending to live]
23. biting
24. condition of being born again
25. able to be spoken to [easy to talk to]
26. falling down
27. being strong in front
28. beginning to be strong together
29. [one] climbing down
30. pushing back
31. condition of jumping back
32. cumbere *to lie* > condition of lying upon
33. latēre *to lie hidden* > condition of lying hidden
34. vilis *cheap, worthless* > make cheap
35. vigilare *be wakeful* > being wakeful
36. delinquere *leave off, be wanting* > condition of being
wanting
37. humēre *be wet/moist* > a. condition of being moist
 b. pertaining to the condition of being moist
 c. tending to be moist
 d. condition of tending to be moist
38. squalēre *to be stiff/clotted*: form words as in 37a-d
39. tumēre *to be swollen*: form words as in 37-38
40. act of looking at from underneath

Chapter six: check list

1. Suffixes added to the present base
    a. Noun-forming
        -or
        -ium, -y
        -ion
        -men
        -ment
        -bulum, -ble
        -culum, -cle

    b. Participial suffixes
        -nt
        -nce, -ncy
        -nd, -ndous

    c. Adjective-forming
        -id
        -ile
        -ble
        -acious
        -ulous
        -uous

    d. Verbal suffixes
        -sc- [-esce, -isce]
        -fy, -fic, -fication
        -igate

Fill in meaning and at least one example of each suffix used in a word.

2. Vocabulary: learn all new words, especially those marked *.

Fill in a derivative of each base given for each verb.

Verb Game

Which does not belong [i.e. which does not share a Latin verb with the others]?

        agent   intransigent   agenda   age   agile
        captor   capacious   incipient   decapitate
        pare   parachute   parallel   preparation
        audacious   auditorium   inaudible   obey
        data   date   addenda   editorial   day
        duke   aqueduct   induction   duck
        repel   pell-mell   impulsive   pulse
        clam   clamor   exclamation   claimant
        chief   receive   incipient   conception
        remittance   omit   emission   miss
        fallacious   infallible   fall   fail

84

Lesson six: Supplement

Some common abbreviations: be able to explain how each is used

i. e. *id est* *that is*

et al. *et alii/et aliae/et alia* [different forms indicate the different genders, masculine, feminine, neuter, respectively] *and others*

etc. *et cetera* *and the others, and so forth*

q. v. *quod vide* *which see*

et seq./et seqq.   *et sequitur/et sequuntur* [the two forms are for singular and plural respectively] *and the following*

op. cit.   [in] *opere citato* *in the work cited*

loc. cit. [in] *loco citato* *in the place cited*

id. *idem* *the same*

ibid.   *ibidem* *in the same place*

N. B.   *nota bene* *note well*

viz.   *videlicet* *it is permitted to see, that is to say, namely*

e. g.   *exempli gratia*   *for example*

        passim *throughout, here and there*

        sic   *thus*

Project: read an article in a learned journal in your field. Be able to explain the use of all the abbreviations used. Make a note of any Latin abbreviations or expressions not on the list above.

Words in Context

The meaning doesn't matter if it's only idle chatter of a
transcendental kind.

W. S. Gilbert

In the constancy of his people he was somewhat *diffident*.

Raleigh

The *docile* mind may soon thy *precepts* know.

Jonson

He regards the enemies of pleasure with *complacency*.

Jowett

Soldiers are citizens of death's grey land
Drawing no *dividend* from time's tomorrows.

Sassoon

More *pellucid* streams
An ampler ether, a diviner air
And fields invested with purpureal gleams.

Wordsworth

Milton

Wee, sleekit, cow'rin', *tim'rous* beastie
O what a panic's in thy breastie.

Burns

The *query* seemed intolerable and *insolent* to the little exquisite
woman in her silken nest, and suddenly, knowing at last that she
was committed to a certain pattern of foolery, and hating the old
witch who had helped her into it, she said in a sweet weak way...

M. F. K. Fisher

She is really getting beyond our management and does not mind us
even when we speak *peremptorily* to her.

Emily Eden

Rise, sir, from this *semi-recumbent* posture.

Oscar Wilde

Lesson Seven: Suffixes added to ppp base

For review of **ppp** bases, work on these direct or simple entries
from ppp bases.

Practice exercise 1:   Give meaning of Latin verb and meaning of
English derivative.

1.   precise
2.   composite
3.   oblate
4.   subject
5.   errata
6.   abrupt
7.   apposite
8.   cognate
9.   erose
10. discrete
11. irresolute
12. exquisite
13. intense
14. transcript
15. interdict
16. separate
17. reject
18. recondite
19. emigrate
20. remorse
21. process
22. devise
23. subtract
24. prefect
25. exempt
26. prerequisite
27. adverse
28. profuse
29. finite [< finire *to limit* < finis]
30. indefinite

Practice exercise 2:   make up one word from the ppp base of each
of these; add prefixes but not suffixes:

1.   movēre/motum [*move*]
2.   jungere/junctum [*join*]
3.   pingere/pictum [*prick, paint*]
4.   torquēre/tortum [*twist*]
5.   tangere/tactum
6.   oriri/ortum [*rise*]
7.   sequi/secutum
8.   vidēre/visum
9.   fluere/fluxum [*flow*]
10. regere/rectum
11. facere/factum [*-fect*]
12. rogare/rogatum

1.   **Noun-forming suffixes added to ppp base**

   -or [Latin -or] *one who, that which*
       narrator < *narrare/narratum, to tell: one who tells*
       sector < *secare/sectum, to cut: that which cuts*

   -ion [Latin -io, -ion-] *an act; the state or result of an
     act*
       vision: *the state of seeing*
       distortion: *the result of twisting in different
         directions*

   -ure [Latin -ura] *the act or result of*
       fracture: *the result of breaking*
       pressure: *the act of squeezing*

   [Latin -us] > -t, -s [= ppp base alone] or ppp base + -e *an
     act or the result of an act*
     Many words using this suffix will show a u in the stem if
     a second suffix is added.
       sense: *act/result of feeling*
       sensual: *concerned with the act of feeling*
       case: *result of falling*
       casual: *connected with act of falling*

Practice exercises 3 using vocabulary words from previous lessons

A.   Take apart and define each part

1.   oblation
2.   actor
3.   detractor
4.   recessional
5.   sensuality
6.   verse
7.   equivocation
8.   scriptural
9.   manumission [*the act of freeing: literally,*_____]
10. interdiction
11. exemption
12. stature
13. tension
14. discretion
15. precursor
16. profession
17. gesture
18. lecture
19. auction
20. circumspection
21. audition
22. stricture
23. nature
24. restriction
25. intermission

26.   circumlocution
27.   contractual
28.   interlocutor
29.   excursion
30.   resolution
31.   collaboration
32.   evacuation
33.   recreational
34.   decapitation [caput, capit-]
35.   incarnational [caro, carn-]
36.   cooperation   [opus, oper-]
37.   perturbation [turba *crowd, disturbance*]
38.   innovation   [novus]
39.   regeneration [genus, gener-]
40.   annihilation [nihil]

B.   Make up words meaning
1.   act of going [use word meaning *go/yield*] between
2.   act of buying back
3.   result of taking to [oneslf]
4.   one who wins
5.   one who teaches
6.   result of breaking
7.   result of snatching
8.   act of moving rapidly in
9.   act of sitting
10.   result of seeing again
11.   one who follows out
12.   result of putting next to

C.   Make up one **agent** [*one who, that which*] and one abstract
[*act, state, condition of being*] from the ppp base of each of
these verbs. Use prefixes; remember vowel reduction.

1.   capere/**captum**
2.   facere/**factum**
3.   agere/**actum**
4.   trahere/**tractum**
5.   quaerere/**quaesitum**
6.   sequi/**secutum**
7.   loqui/**locutum**
8.   audire/**auditum**
9.   ducere/**ductum**

D.   Review suffixes added to present base and make up one
abstract using each base

Example: loqui, locutum present: **eloquence**; ppp: circumlocution

1.   frangere (frag-)/fractum
2.   regere/rectum
3.   specere/spectum
4.   legere/lectum
5.   tendere/tentum, tensum
6.   currere/cursum

2. Adjective-forming suffixes added to ppp base

-ile [Latin -ilis] able to be
    ductile: able to be drawn, led
    missile: [something] that can be sent

-ible [Latin -ibilis] able to be
    comprehensible: able to be understood
    plausible [< plaudere, plausum clap, approve] able to
      be approved, deserving applause

-ory, -orious, -orial [Latin -orius] pertaining to
    auditory pertaining to/concerned with hearing

-ive [Latin -ivus] tending to
    active tending to do
    jussive [< jubēre/jussum command] tending to command

Practice exercise 4:

A. Take apart; give meaning of verb stem, define suffix.

1. reactive
2. native
3. concessive
4. exclamatory
5. migratory
6. ductile
7. productive
8. relative
9. submissive
10. preparatory
11. proscriptive
12. sensible
13. evocative
14. redemptive
15. contradictory
16. elusive
17. positive
18. prehensile
19. inquisitive
20. derogatory
21. evasive
22. corrective
23. tactile
24. consecutive
25. executive

B. Make up words meaning

1. tending to lead/draw in
2. tending to weigh
3. tending to run
4. tending to save in advance

3. Frequentatives

Frequentatives are verbs formed from verbs. They express *constant, repeated* or *intensified* action. Frequentatives are formed from the ppp base, by adding *first conjugation endings*, that is add -are, -atum to the ppp base.
[Sometimes -itare, -itatum is added instead.]

> **gestate** <gerere, gestum *carry*: *to carry constantly*
> **hesitate** <haerēre, haesitum *stick*: *to keep sticking*

Practice exercise 5: Identify verb, give meaning of compound

1. incantation
2. visitation
3   cessation
4. gestation
5. dictate
6. agitate
7. tentative
8. conversation
9. pulsate
10. expectation
11. spectator
12. sensation
13. habitation
14. tractate

Practice exercise 6: Tell which are **frequentatives**, which are **inchoatives**, and which are **denominatives**; identify the base of each and give its meaning. Give meaning of the whole compound.

Example: denominative: is a <u>denominative</u>
         base: *nomen, nomin-* <u>name</u>
         meaning: *tending to be made from nouns/names*

        inchoative: also a <u>denominative</u>
         base: *choum/cohum* <u>a strap attaching the yoke to the plow</u> i.e. something used for the first step
         meaning: *tending to make a beginning*

1. incandescent
2. dictation
3. animate
4. elaborate
5. agitation
6. alienate
7. convalesce
8. crescent
9. hesitation
10. peroration
11. obliterate
12. obsolescence
13. pulsating
14. finish

Vocabulary: Learn these, especially those marked *

aperire, apertum *open*
* censēre, censum *assess, rate, estimate*
* colere, cultum *till, honor, dwell*
* credere, creditum *believe*
-fendere, -fensum *strike, hurt*
findere, fissum *split*
fingere, fictum *form*
fugere, fugitum *flee*
fungi, functum *perform*
* gradi (-gred-), gressum *step, walk*
* habēre, habitum *have, hold*
imitari, imitatum *copy*
* jungere, junctum *join*
labi, lapsum *slip*
* monēre, monitum *warn*
* movēre, motum *move*
pingere (pig-), pictum *mark by incision, tatoo, paint*
pungere, punctum *prick, sting*
rēri, ratum *think*
stinguere, stinctum *quench*
struere, structum *pile up, build*
tegere, tectum *cover*
* texere, textum *weave, build*
tingere, tinctum *dip*
tondere, tonsum *shear, clip, shave*
* torquēre (tor-), tortum *twist*
vellere, vulsum *pluck, pull*
vexare, vexatum *shake*
vovēre, votum *vow, promise*

Exercise 1: using new vocabulary and new suffixes form one **agent**
and one **abstract** from each of the following [use *-or* and *-ion* or
-ure]. Use prefixes if necessary.

Example: movēre/motum: agent **motor**;   abstracts   **motion**,
promotion, commotion, demotion, emotion

1. monēre
2. censēre
3. imitari
4. struere
5. tegere
6. gradi

Exercise 2:   noun and adjective: make up one noun in *-ion/-ure*
and one adjective in *-ive, -ile* or *-ory*

Example: movēre/motum: noun **motion**; adjectives **motive, emotive**

Fill in ppp

1. jungere
2. monēre

3. vellere
4. tegere
5. stinguere
6. findere
7. fungi
8. gradi
9. rumpere
10. pellere
11. agere
12. capere
13. fundere
14. ponere
15. dicere
16. emere
17. specere
18. tendere
19. sequi
20. ducere

Exercise 3:   Make up words meaning

1. act of twisting out
2. act of warning in advance
3. result of joining together
4. tending to pile down
5. result of painting
6. tending to flee
7. one who estimates
8. tending to walk to [or against]
9. result of having continuously
10. tending to perform through
11. tending to believe [use present base]
12. not able to be believed

Exercise 4:   Take apart and define

1. defunct
2. habile
3. aperture
4. censorious
5. credulous
6. credible
7. fictile
8. figment
9. labile
10. tincture
11. depictive
12. offensive
13. fissure
14. dereliction   [linquere, lictum *leave*]
15. culture
16. puncture
17. compunction

18. junction
19. disjunctive
20. destruction
21. constructive
22. restructure
23. votive
24. devotion
25. tonsure
26. commotion
27. protective
28. detector
29. revulsion
30. comprehensive
31. comprehensible
32. fissile
33. extrasensory perception

Exercise 4:Make up one adjective each from the present base and
the ppp base.

Example: **sequi/secutum** pres. *subsequent*; ppp *consecutive*

1.   legere/lectum
2.   agere/actum
3.   facere/factum
4.   sentire/sensum
5.   loqui/locutum
6.   cedere/cessum
7.   venire/ventum
8.   gradi/gressum
9.   capere/captum
10.   petere/petitum
11.   nasci/natum
12.   stringere/strictum
13.   tangere/tactum
14.   vidēre/visum
15.   fari/fatum

Exercise 5: Make up one noun from each base

Example: **agere** pres. *agenda*; ppp *actor, action, activity*

1.   torquēre/tortum [pres. combining base: **tor-**]
2.   tendere/tensum,tentum
3.   stare/statum
4.   vidēre/visum
5.   loqui/locutum
6.   pingere/pictum [pres. base: **pig-**]
7.   augēre/auctum
8.   sentire/sensum
9.   currere/cursum
10.   capere/captum
11.   trahere/tractum
12.   mittere/missum
13.   legere/lectum

94

Lesson seven: check list

1. Suffixes added to ppp base Fill in meanings and examples

> Noun-forming suffixes

>> -or
>> -ion
>> -ure
>> [-tus/-sus]

> Adjective-forming suffixes

>> -ile
>> -ible
>> -orious, -ory, -orial
>> -ive

> Verb forming suffix: *Frequentative*
>> -at-, -it-

2. Vocabulary: Concentrate on these

> censēre, censum
> colere, cultum
> credere, creditum
> gradī, gressum
> habēre, habitum
> jungere, junctum
> movēre, motum
> monēre, monitum
> struere, structum
> texere, textum
> torquēre, tortum

Explain these words

censorship
cultivated
creed
graduate
habitat
enjoin
movie
money
construe
textual/textural
retort

Supplement for lesson seven: Verb review

1. Suffixes: fill in meaning, tell which base(s) is (are) used, give an example:

Noun-forming suffixes

        -ion [pres. base]
                    [ppp]
        -or [pres. base]
                    [ppp]
        -ble
        -cle
        -cide [added to noun-base]
        -nce, -ncy
        -men
        -ment
        -ium, -y
        -ure
        [-tus/-sus]

Adjective-forming suffixes

        -acious
        -id
        -ble
        -fic [added to adj., noun bases]
        -ile
        -ive
        -ndous
        -nt
        -orious, -ory
        -ulous
        -uous

Verb-forming suffixes

        -ate [to noun bases]
        -ate [to ppp bases]
        -sc-
        -fy
        -igate

2. **Most productive verbs:** give ten derivatives of each; choose one and find thirty derivatives

    1. agere/actum
    2. capere/captum
    3. ducere/ductum
    4. dicere/dictum
    5. gerere/gestum
    6. facere/factum
    7. cedere/cessum
    8. mittere/missum
    9. venire/ventum
    10. tenēre/tentum
    11. legere/lectum
    12. vertere/versum
    13. stare/statum
    14. regere/rectum
    15. vidēre/visum
    16. portare/portatum
    17. ferre/latum
    18. ponere/positum
    19. specere/spectum
    20. tendere/tentum, tensum

Fill in meanings of all.

Choose one and answer these questions:

1. What are the two stems?
2. Is this an -i-stem?
3. Does this verb show vowel reduction?
4. Does it have any unusual stems in English?
5. List thirty derivatives (if possible fifty).

Example: **capere/captum** *take, seize*
    1. cap(i)-/capt-
    2. yes, it is an -i-stem.
    3. yes, -cipi-, -cept-
    4. yes, it has forms in -ceive
    5. capacious   captor   caption   captive   captivate
        captivity   capacity   deceive   deceit   incapacitate
        deception   deceptive conceive   concept   incipient
        inception   inceptive capture   perceive   conceivable
        precept   preceptor except   exception inconceivable
        conception   accept   capable   incapable contraception
        conceptual   intercept receive   recipient imperceptible
        acceptance   reception receptive recapture contraceptive
        receptacle   principal principle participle participial
        misconception   participate   participatory
        acceptable   susceptible anticipate   perception
        perceptive   exceptional

    6. some unusal derivatives: prince purchase cater
        cable   caitiff   capstan   catch   emancipate
        chase   conceit   occupy   recipe   recuperate

97

3. Other important verbs: give meanings and five derivatives of each

1. audire/auditum
2. augēre/auctum
3. cadere/casum
4. caedere/caesum
5. cernere/cretum
6. claudere/clausum
7. colere/cultum
8. currere/cursum
9. dare/datum
10. emere/emptum
11. findere/fissum
12. fingere/fictum
13. fari/fatum
14. frangere/fractum
15. fundere/fusum
16. fungi/functum
17. haerēre/haesum, haesitare [freq.]
18. ire/itum
19. jacere/jactum
20. jungere/junctum
21. manēre, mansum
22. migrare/migratum
23. monēre/monitum
24. movēre/motum
25. mutare/mutatum
26. nasci/natum
27. pati/passum *suffer*
28. pellere/pulsum
29. pendere/pensum
30. petere/petitum
31. ponere/positum
32. prehendere/prehensum
33. premere/pressum
34. quaerere/quaesitum
35. rapere/raptum
36. rēri, ratum
37. scandere/scansum
38. scire [scitum]
39. sedēre/sessum
40. sentire/sensum
41. sequi/secutum
42. solvere/solutum
43. struere/structum
44. sumere/sumptum
45. tangere/tactum
46. torquēre/tortum
47. trahere/tractum
48. trudere/trusum *thrust*
49. uti/usum
50. vincere/victum
51. vivere/victum
52. volvere/volutum

Word Game: Add a Letter

Example: w o r d   w o r l d   clues: *verbum, the cosmos*

1. _ _ _ _ _ _   to establish as true
    _ _ _ _ _ _ _   to write poetry

2. _ _ _ _ _   a sign of the zodiac
    _ _ _ _ _ _   a heroic woman; a domineering woman

3. _ _ _ _   dare or resist
    _ _ _ _ _   to turn into a god

4. _ _ _ _   volcanic rock
    _ _ _ _ _   insect stage

5. _ _ _ _ _   express happiness
    _ _ _ _ _ _   likeness

6. _ _ _ _ _ _   plump
    _ _ _ _ _ _ _   magniloquent

7. _ _ _ _ _   ethical
    _ _ _ _ _ _   deadly

8. _ _ _ _   genuine
    _ _ _ _ _   kingly
    _ _ _ _ _ _   entertain

9. _ _ _ _ _ _ _   a small joint
    _ _ _ _ _ _ _ _   a small piece

10. _ _ _ _   meat of calf
    _ _ _ _ _   for sale

11. _ _ _ _ _   a press of people
    _ _ _ _ _ _   boasted

12. _ _ _ _ _   did one's sums
    _ _ _ _ _ _   confused

13. _ _ _ _ _   have fun
    _ _ _ _ _ _   make manifest

14. _ _ _ _ _   respond
    _ _ _ _ _ _   edit

15. _ _ _ _ _ _   freeing
    _ _ _ _ _ _ _   enigmatic

16. _ _ _ _ _ _   used to
    _ _ _ _ _ _ _   hurt

17. _ _ _ _ _ _ _ _   charged with a crime
    _ _ _ _ _ _ _ _ _   pointed out

"I do not think," said Sir Edgar, and his old cracked voice was additionally broken with emotion, "that the Association has been privileged for a very long time to hear a speech at once so learned and so humane as the one we have heard this evening. Professor Pforzheim, in his survey of Dark Age and Early Medieval trade, has taken us on a vast geographical journey from Canton to the shores of the Iberian Peninsula, and from the Baltic to the Upper Nile; but he has taken me, and I dare say, many of you on an even wider spiritual journey, for he has recalled, to me at any rate, a time when historical studies demanded, as their simple *prerequisites*, learning lightly worn, high courage of imagination, and strong intellectual discipline."

> Angus Wilson,
> *Anglo-Saxon Attitudes*

While Rosskam went for the junk alone, Francis stared across the street and saw his mother in housedress and apron *surreptitiously* throwing salt on the roots of the young maple tree that grew in the Daugherty yard but had the *temerity* to drop twigs, leaves and pods onto the Phelan tomato plants and flowers.

> William Kennedy,
> *Ironweed*

And there, in his office, where he had hoped to sit down and mope quietly about his failure, had been Bevill Higgin, who had introduced himself with the most ridiculous *affectation* of what he considered to be a university manner, and who had proposed that he, Solly, should permit Higgin to give readings from English poetry to his classes, in order, as Higgin put it, to give them the *sonorous* roll of the verse and to *illuminate* what had, it was *implied*, been presented to them in a dull and lifeless manner. To make his meaning perfectly clear he had *declaimed* a few lines of Satan's Address to the Sun, in an embarrassing, *elocutionary* manner, like a man trying out his voice in a bathroom.

> Robertson Davies,
> *Leaven of Malice*

Chapter Eight: Greek words into English

   Greek,   like   Latin   is   an   inflected   language.   The
explanations of case, declensions, verbs, conjugations, principal
parts,   and   so forth,   need not be repeated.   Greek   nouns   and
adjectives belong   to   three   declensions   with   the   third   (or
consonant declension) often showing a change in the nominative so
that a second combining form (or base) will be given.   The Greek
verb   is   even more complex than the Latin,   often showing   vowel
changes in the various tenses: the important variations in   the
stem will be given with each verb.

   Since   Greek   is written in a different alphabet than   Latin
and English,   before Greek words can be borrowed they must   first
be   *transliterated*,   that is,   changed from one alphabet into   the
other.   It is traditional to change the Greek words into   Latin,
to   make them conform to Latin spelling conventions.   There   is,
however,   no   entirely   consistent   method   of   transliteration
(especially   of Greek names) universally followed by   writers   of
English,   so   that,   for   example,   the   name   *Aeschylus*   [Latin
spelling] will be seen as *Aischulos* or even *Aiskhulos*,   depending
on the taste of the writer or editor.   Many writers on classical
Greek literature,   history,   or culture prefer the spelling that is
closest   to   the   original Greek in sound and appearance   and   so
choose to write the name of the "father of tragedy" in one of the
latter two forms.

   The Greek words in these lessons will be given in the   Roman
alphabet in the transliteration closest to the Greek original (as
in the second example, *Aischulos*.   At the end of this   lesson the
supplement will give some explanations and exercises on the Greek
alphabet and using the Greek dictionary.

**Rules for making Greek words conform to Latin orthographical and
morphological conventions [i.e. rules of spelling and grammar]**

       k   > c
       u   > y [except in diphthongs: *au, eu* > *au, eu*]
       ai > ae > e [Latin *ae* usually becomes English *e*]
       ei > e or i
       oi > oe > e or i
       ou > u

       -os   > -us
       -on   > -um
       -ōn sometimes > -o
       -ē   sometimes > -a

Others   will   be treated in the supplement to   this   lesson.   In
proper names the Latin spelling is commonly retained,   especially
for well known persons.   For less famous individuals either   the
Latin   spelling   or   an   approximation of the Greek (with   many
variations)   may   be   used.   For   example,   Platōn   is   almost

universally spelled *Plato* in English [but cf. Italian *Platone*, French *Platon*, Spanish *Platon*]. Another Greek name is variously spelled Euclid when referring to the famous geometer and Euclides, Eukleides when referring to other persons of that name.

Exercise 1:   Change into Latin spellings and give English derivative.

Example: *etumologia*,   Latin *etymologia*,   English **etymology** [remember that Latin −*ia* > English −y] Be sure you know what the word *etymology* means.

1.   krisis
2.   ainigma
3.   daimōn
4.   dunamis
5.   korōnē
6.   Kritōn [a good friend of Platon]
7.   Mousa [one of nine]
8.   phoinix
9.   phainomena [plural of phainomenon *thing seen*]
10. papuros
11. psuchē
12. thēsauros [*treasure*]
13. kalux
14. gumnasion
15. Kithairōn   [a mountain near Thebes, famous in song and story]

Proper names: transliterate and identify briefly

1.   Sophoklēs
2.   Sōkratēs
3.   Thoukudidēs
4.   Epikouros
5.   Hēsiodos
6.   Aischulos
7.   Alkibiadēs
8.   Periklēs
9.   Apollōn
10. Bakchos
11. Delphoi
12. Surakousai
13. Thermopulai
14. Aiguptos

Changing Greek words into English: Greek words come into English
in the same ways Latin words do.

1. No change (except in alphabet)
    hubris: violence, excessive arrogance, hubris
    agapē: love, agape
    echō: sound, echo   [see if you can find the story of the
        nymph Echo and her love for Narcissus]

2. The base alone becomes the English word
    dicastēs: member of the jury, judge, dicast
    humnos: song, hymn
    puxis: boxwood, box, pyx
    diaita: way of living, diet

3. The base + silent -e
    thumos: an aromatic herb, thyme
    proselutos: one who comes to a place, proselyte
    sphaira: a ball, sphere

4. Changes of endings
    -ia > -y   *etumologia* > etymology
    -eia > -ia > -y   *politeia* > polity
    -tia > -cy   *demokratia* > democracy

5. Irregular changes
    hōra, time > hour
    scholē, leisure > school
    turannos, king > tyrant
    eleēmosunē, mercy, pity > alms [cf. eleemosynary]

Exercise 2: Change these to English words

Example: axioma [that which is thought worthy] > axiom [base
alone]

1.   thēma [something set, placed]
2.   anathēma [something set up]
3.   ergon [work]
4.   skēnē [tent]
5.   kuklos [circle]
6.   Akadēmeia [Plato's school]
7.   theatron [place for viewing]
8.   sukophantēs [informer]
9.   agora [marketplace]
10. angelos [messenger]
11. biblion [book]
12. diakonos [servant, attendant]
13. eirōneia [affected ignorance]
14. historia [inquiry]
15. lura [stringed instrument]
16. pompē [a sending > a solemn procession]
17. aiōn [age]

18. tupos [mark]
19. ekleipsis [a leaving out]
20. thronos [armchair]
21. drakōn [serpent]

Vocabulary   learn these

aēr   *air*
angelos   *messenger*
anthrōpos   *human being*
astēr   *star*
axios   *worthy*
biblion   *book*
bios   *life*
chrōma, chromat-   *color*
daimōn   *spirit, divinity*
eikōn   *image, likeness*
ergon   *work*
ethos   *custom*
hōra   *time, hour*
kosmos   *order, universe, adornment*
kuklos   *circle*
logos   *word, reason*
metron   *measure*
mimos   *imitator*
philos   *beloved, dear, loving*
phōnē   *voice*
phōs, phōt-   *light*
scholē   *leisure*
sophos   *wise*
theos   *god*
tupos   *mark*

Exercise 3:   Give two or more English derivatives of each of the
new vocabulary words.

Example: *ergon* > erg, energy, synergy, ergophobia, ergometer,
allergy, demiurge, dramaturgical, liturgy, liturgics, georgic,
metallurgy, synergism, surgery, thaumaturgy

biblion   > Bible,   bibliography,   bibliolater,   bibliophile,
biblioklept, gymnobiblist, biblical, bibliophobe, bibliomania,
bibliomancy, bibliopole, bibliotics, bibliotheca [cf. French,
bibliotheque]

Check list

1.   Transliteration: give Roman spellings of: k   u   ai   ei   ou
oi -os -on -eia

2.   Simple changes: list the "rules".

3.   Review vocabulary

Supplement to chapter eight: The Greek alphabet

Greek character		Name	Transliteration		Pronunciation
α	A	alpha	a		short: cup; long: father
β	B	beta	b		b
γ	Γ	gamma	g, ng		hard, go; ng before g/k/ch
δ	Δ	delta	d		d
ε	E	epsilon	e		short e: bet
ζ	Z	zeta	z		sd: wisdom
η	H	eta	e		long e: ate
θ	Θ	theta	th		thing [or t-h]
ι	I	iota	i		short: tin; long: teen
κ	K	kappa	k, c		k
λ	Λ	lambda	l		l
μ	M	mu	m		m
ν	N	nu	n		n
ξ	Ξ	xi	x		ks, x
ο	O	omicron	o		short o: pot
π	Π	pi	p		p
ρ	P	rho	r, rh		trilled r
σ ς	Σ	sigma	s		s
τ	T	tau	t		t
υ	Υ	upsilon	y, u		French u
φ	Φ	phi	ph		phone [or p-h]
χ	X	chi	ch		loch [or c-h]
ω	Ω	omega	o		long o: go

The symbol ' is not transliterated, but ' stands for the letter h.

Diphthongs:

αι	> ai, ae, e
αυ	> au
ει	> ei, e, i
οι	> oi, oe, e, i
ου	> u, ou
ευ	> eu

Practice exercises

A.   Transliterate into the Roman alphabet and give one English derivative:

1. ἄγγελος
2. ἀστήρ
3. ἄξιος
4. βιβλίον
5. χρῶμα
6. δαίμων

7. εἰκών
8. ἔργον
9. ἦθος
10. ὥρα
11. κόσμος
12. κύκλος
13. μέτρον
14. φωνή
15. σχολή
16. τύπος

B. Put these into Greek

1. Aspasia
2. Sapphō
3. Xanthippē
4. Antigonē
5. Ēlectra [first e is long]

C. Transliterate these [choose five and identify them]

1. Κλυταιμνῆστρα
2. Κασσάνδρα
3. Μηδεία
4. Ἀνδρομάχη
5. Ἀστυάναξ
6. Ἕκτωρ
7. Ἀχιλλεύς
8. Ὅμηρος
9. Ἄλκηστις
10. Ἀπόλλων
11. Ἰάσων
12. Διόνυσος
13. Ἱππόλυτος
14. Φαίδρα
15. Θησεύς
16. Ἀφροδίτη
17. Ἥρα
18. Ἄρτεμις
19. Ἑκάβη
20. Ἑρμιόνη
21. Ἰφιγένεια
    Ἑλένη

D. Put into Greek letters:

1. chronos *time*
2. philos *loving, dear*
3. gunē *woman*
4. anēr *man*
5. anthrōpos *human being*
6. dēmos *the people*
7. dendron *tree*

8. hēlios *the sun*
9. lithos *stone*
10. xenos *stranger*
11. theos *a god, God*
12. zōon *living thing, animal*
13. bios *life*
14. mētēr *mother*
15. metron *measure*
16. ploutos *wealth*
17. sōma *body*
18. psuchē *soul*
19. logos *word, reason*
20. rhopalon *club* [cf. rhopalic]
21. hulē *wood, material*

Optional: Look up one of these words in a Classical Greek
lexicon. The breathing mark [*h* sound] does not affect
alphabetical order. [Look up *hule* under u, upsilon.]

Word game: Letter hunt

Find the names of letters in these words:

    alphabet
    abecedarium
    iotacism
    chiasmus
    rhotacism
    gamma rays
    delta [as Mississippi delta]
    zed
    jot
    lambdoid
    sigmoid flexure
    tau cross
    alpha and omega
    betatron
    lambda particle
    alphanumeric
    Phi Beta Kappa
    asigmatic
    chiasma

What is Y called in French?
What is the formula for the circumference of a circle?   for the
area of a circle?

Nor shall this peace sleep with her; but as when
The bird of wonder dies, the maiden *phoenix*,
Her ashes new-create another heir
As great in admiration as herself.

Shakespeare

Ride on! ride on in majesty!
In lowly *pomp* ride on to die.

Henry Milman

Clap an extinguisher on your *irony*, if you are unhappily blessed
with a vein of it.

Charles Lamb

His locked, letter'd, braw brass collar
Shew'd him the gentleman and *scholar*.

Robert Burns

Let him be *Anathema*, Maran-atha.

St. Paul

A person both God and Man, an *enigma* [aenigma] to all Nations and
to all Sciences.

J. Taylor

The *calyx* is nothing but the swaddling clothes of the flower.
Ruskin

The few rolls of *papyrus* which the ancients deemed a notable
collection of books...

Lytton

What the energetic *pleonasm* of our ancestors called "a false
lie". [1860]

Tobacco, divine, rare, superexcellent tobacco, which goes far
beyond all their *panaceas*, potable gold, and philosopher's
stones, a sovereign remedy to all diseases...But as it is
commonly abused by most men... 'tis a plague, a mischief
of body and soul.

Robert Burton

Chapter Nine: Compounds from two Greek noun bases

Many derivatives from Greek are formed from two noun bases. In such compounds one element usually depends on the other in a genitive or adjectival relationship.

misology   hatred of reason
skiaphobia   fear of shadows
archbishop   first [highest ranking] bishop

The most common connecting vowel in such compounds is -o-; but -a- is sometimes used in compounds having a first declension noun as first element. Nouns of the third declension sometimes retain their own stem vowel but often drop it and add -o-.

Study this list of words commonly used as elements in compounds. Learn any marked *.

* philo- [Greek, philos, loving, dear] love of
        philology, love of logos
   *-phile one loving
        bibliophile, lover of books
   -philous, -philic tending to love
   -philia; -philiac love of > tendency toward > abnormal
        attraction to; one abnormally attracted to

* miso- [Greek, misos, hatred] hate of
        misology, hatred of logos

* -meter [Greek, metron, measure] an instrument for measuring
        thermometer, an instrument for measuring heat

* -phone [Greek, phōnē, voice] sound, sound emitting device
        telephone, device for emitting sound from far away

-latry [Greek, latreia service for pay] worship of
        idolatry, worship of idols
   -later worshipper of
   -latrous tending to worship

* -logy [Greek logos, word] discourse, speech, the science,
        theory, study of
        anthropology, the study of mankind

-phobia [Greek phobos, fear] fear of
        agoraphobia fear of the marketplace/open places
   -phobe one who fears: skiaphobe one who fears shadows

-nomy [Greek nomos, law, custom, usage] systematized knowledge
        of, laws concerning
        astronomy systematized study of the stars

-scope [Greek skopein, to look at] instrument for observing
        telescope instrument for observing from afar

-some [Greek sōma, body] *body*
        chromosome *color body*

-gony [Greek *goneia*, generation < *gonos*, offspring, seed]
        production of
        cosmogony *production/creation of the universe*

-genesis [Greek, *genesis*, birth, origin] *generation, birth*
        parthenogenesis *virgin birth*

* -onym [Greek *onoma*, name] *name*
        pseudonym *false name*

-mancy [Greek *manteia*, prophecy] *telling the future by*
        necromancy *divination by means of dead bodies/ghosts*

-cracy [Greek *kratia*, strength, power] *government by*
        democracy *government by the people*

-iatry [Greek *iatreia*, healing] *medical treatment*
        psychiatry *medical treatment of soul/mind*

* -graphy [Greek *graphein*, to write] *a method of writing; a*
        descriptive science
        iconography *method of drawing images*
        geography *descriptive science of the earth*

    -graph *means of writing/drawing; something drawn/written*
    -graphic *having to do with method of writing / descriptive*
        science
    -grapher *one who writes about a field; one who uses a*
        specific means of writing or drawing

* -archy [Greek *archē*, rule] *government, rule*
        monarchy *rule by one*

-mania [Greek *mania*, madness] *madness, exaggerated craving*
        bibliomania *excessive craving for books*
        -maniac *one displaying such an excessive craving*

Exercise 1:   Using the vocabulary from the previous lesson, make
up words meaning:

    1.   one who fears books
    2.   systematized knowledge of work
    3.   study of marks
    4.   drawing of images
    5.   instrument to measure rings
    6.   worship of demons
    7.   instrument for looking at the hour [of birth]
    8.   divination by stars
    9.   rule by imitators
    10. the production of colors
    11. excessive craving for voices

110

Exercise 2:   What do these mean?

1. ethology
2. astrology
3. astronomy
4. bibliography
5. ergophobia
6. cosmology
7. typography
8. chromatometer
9. axiology
10. mimomania
11. cyclophobia
12. metrophile
13. iconolatry
14. angelography
15. ergomania
16. demonocracy
17. misobiblist
18. misologist
19. misanthrope
20. philanthropist
21. mimeograph
22. cosmography
23. ergonomy
24. chromatography
25. astrogenesis

Exercise 3:   make   up fifty -logies: if you run out   use   the
glossary.   Know what the subject of each -logy is.

Optional exercise: what do these fear?

triskaidekaphobe
skiaphobe
scotophobe
nyctophobe
hypnophobe
trichophobe
demophobe
demonophobe
cynophobe
capnophobe
pyrophobe
photophobe
heliophobe
xylophobe
dendrophobe
anthophobe
anthropophobe
agoraphobe
phobophobe
pantophobe

Vocabulary: study these; learn any marked *

* aitia [etio-] cause
algos [-algia] pain
anemos wind [cf. Latin, animus/anima, breath, spirit]
* anthrōpos human being
anēr, andr- man (male)
atmos steam, vapor
* bios life
* chronos time
dēmos the people
dendron tree
ethnos nation, people
gamos marriage, sexual union
* gē [geo-] earth
glōssa/glōtta tongue, language
* gunē, gunaik- woman
haima, haimat- [hem-/hemat-] blood
hēlios the sun
histos web, tissue
* hudōr, hydro- water
hypsos height
ichthus fish
karpos fruit
kephalē head
kruos [cryo-] frost
* lithos stone
lukos wolf
martur witness
* mētēr, metro- mother
* morphē shape, form
muthos speech, story
naus ship   -naut, sailor
nekros corpse
nephos cloud
* oikos [eco-] house, environment
ornis, ornitho- bird
oros mountain
osteon bone
* pais, paid- [ped-] child
* patēr, patro- father
* pathos suffering, experience   -pathy illness
petra rock
phōs, phōto- light
plutus wealth
* polis city, city-state
pous, pod- foot
* psychē soul, breath, life
pur fire
rhiza root
skia shadow
* sōma, sōmato- body
stethos chest
stichos line, verse
taphos tomb

112

tekton [-tect]   *carpenter, builder*
technē   *art, skill*
* telos [teleo-]   *end*
* theos   *god*
therapōn/theraps   *attendant*   therapeia   *treatment*
tokos   *birth*
topos   *place*
xenos   *foreigner, stranger*
xulon   *wood*
* zōon   *animal, living thing*

Exercise 4:   Make up two or more words using each of the new
vocabulary words.

Exercise 5

A.   Take apart and define or use in a sentence:

 1.   etiology
 2.   neuralgia [*neuron*, nerve]
 3.   anemometer
 4.   anthropomorphic
 5.   androgyny
 6.   atmometer
 7.   biography
 8.   dendrochronology
 9.   ethnocentric
10.   misogamy
11.   geometrical
12.   glossalgia
13.   gyniatric
14.   demophobia
15.   hemophilia
16.   heliograph
17.   histopathology
18.   hydromancy
19.   ichthyornis
20.   carpomania
21.   hydrocephalous
22.   cryoscope
23.   lithograph
24.   martyrology
25.   metropolis
26.   geomorphology
27.   mythomania
28.   cosmonaut
29.   necropolis
30.   economy
31.   ornithocracy
32.   orogeny
33.   nephelolater
34.   osteopath
35.   pediatry
36.   patriarch

113

37. psychopath
38. petroglyph [*gluphein* carve]
39. photography
40. plutonomy
41. cosmopolis
42. podiatry
43. psychosomatic
44. rhizomorph
45. pyromancy
46. skiagraphy
47. chromosome
48. stethoscope
49. technocrat
50. stichomythia
51. teleological
52. theocracy
53. cryotherapy
54. Theotokos
55. topolatry
56. xylography
57. xenophile
58. zoogeography
59. xenoglossy
60. gynocracy

B. Make up words meaning:

1. one who hates human beings
2. wolf-man [werewolf]
3. government by wealth
4. animal lover
5. wood-voice
6. line measurement
7. light-writing
8. one who fears shadows
9. government by the people
10. study of fish
11. study of the house
12. treatment by the sun
13. worship of steam
14. fear of strangers
15. instrument for measuring time

C. Give five or more words from each of the following:

1. bios
2. zōon
3. gē
4. psuchē
5. polis
6. sōma
7. ichthus
8. chronos

114

D. Give meaning of base word(s):

Example: *oread*, base *oros*, mountain [oread, mountain nymph]

1.   anemone
2.   gamete
3.   philodendron
4.   hematoma
5.   glossalalia
6.   gynaeceum
7.   helium
8.   morpheme
9.   ecumenical
10. patriot
11. phosphate
12. petroleum
13. pedagogue
14. empyreal
15. enthusiasm [en + theos]
16. hydra
17. teleost

Optional: Guess what bases these are hiding:

18. pew
19. squirrel
20. licorice
21. parsley
22. diocese
23. parish
24. talisman

E. Give examples of:

1.   an etiological myth or story
2.   anthropomorphism
3.   a gloss
4.   a patronymic
5.   a matronymic
6.   a plutomaniac
7.   a megalopolis
8.   stichomythia

Check list

1.   Common compounding nouns

2.   New Vocabulary

Supplement for Lesson Nine

Words from Greek mythology and culture

1. Explain why:

The House of Atreus is not a good name for a family-style restaurant.

Leda and the Swan, Europa and the Bull, Pasiphae's Pet are not proper titles for children's books about people and animals.

The *Oresteia* might not be well received on Mothers' Day.

Aulis may not be the ideal spot for a father/daughter reunion.

Perseus (in John Barth's *Chimera*) is credited with founding and filling the first sculpture museum.

Cronus had gastralgia on his youngest son's birthday.

An aircraft named *Icarus* does not inspire confidence.

2. What are these:

The Judgment of Paris
The Wrath of Achilles
The Labors of Heracles
Penelope's Web
The Seven against Thebes
Philoctetes' Cave
The Sirens' Song
The Sphinx's Riddle
Achilles' Heel
A Procrustean Bed
Midas' Touch
Amazonomachy
Batrachomyomachy
Nephelococcygia

3. In Search of...   Find twelve Olympian Gods in this puzzle:

```
O R E H N O E H T N A P Z E G
A L M A H E P H A E S T U S O
P O S I E D E E P R A E E E H
H E U Z R R N R P O T Z S R C
R E T E M E D A O S H E P A R
O L P E A P O L L O E U M H A
D O S O N I E D O P N S I I E
I B A A L A S A T N A A N A S
T H E M E S U S Y N O I D R D
E X N O D I E S O P G D R A S
```

Chapter Ten: Greek Adjectives used in English

Study these Greek adjectives. They are mostly used as first
elements in compounds.   Learn those marked *.

akros [acro-] *topmost*
* allos [allo-] *other*
aristos [aristo-] *best*
* autos [auto-] *self*
axios [axio-] *worthy*
barus [bary-, bari-, baro-] *heavy*
bathus [bathy-, batho-] *deep*
brachus [brachy-] *short*
etumos [etymo-] *true*
eurus [eury-] *wide*
gumnos [gymno-] *naked*
* heteros [hetero-] *other, one of two*
hieros [hiero-] *holy*
* holos [holo-] *whole*
homos [homo-] *one and the same*
homoios [homeo-, homoio-] *like*
hugros [hygro-] *wet, moist*
* idios [idio-] *one's own, peculiar*
* isos [iso-] *equal*
* kainos [ceno-, caeno-; -cene] *new*
kakos [caco-] *bad, ugly*
kalos [kal-, calo-, calli-] *beautiful*
kenos [ken-, ceno-] *empty*
koinos [ceno-, coeno-] *common*
* makros [macro-] *long*
* megas, megal- [mega-, megalo-; -megaly] *big*
* mikros [micro-] *small*
* monos [mono-] *alone, only, single*
murios [myrio-] *countless, 10, 000*
* neos [neo-] *new*
oligos [oligo-] *few*
orthos [ortho-] *straight*
oxus [oxy-] *sharp*
* palaios [paleo-, palaeo-] *old*
* pas, pant- [pan-, panto-] *all*
platus [platy-] *wide, broad*
* polus [poly-] *much, many*
    pleion [plio-, pleo-] *more, greater*
    pleistos [pleisto-] *most, greatest*
* protos [proto-] *first*
* pseudes [pseudo-] *false*
* sophos [sopho-; -sophy] *wise, clever*
stenos [steno-] *narrow*
stereos [stereo-] *solid, firm*
* tēle [tele-] *far away* {adverb}
thermos [thermo-] *warm, hot*
trachus [trach-, trachy-] *rugged, harsh*
xeros [xero-] *dry*

117

Exercise 1: Form words meaning

1. fear of high places [= topmost things]
2. other writing [i.e. a signature made by one person for another]
3. rule by the "best"
4. self law [i.e. the quality of being self-governing]
5. instrument for measuring weight [pressure]
6. deep rock
7. short foot
8. truth of words
9. priestly [holy] government
10. whole writing
11. peculiar suffering
12. of equal time [equal in duration]
13. recent birth or generation
14. naked seed [seed =*sperma*]
15. of other shape
16. of the same kind
17. instrument for measuring humidity
18. peculiar suffering
19. ugly sound
20. new word usage [usage = *-ism*]
21. empty tomb
22. large o
23. small universe
24. single rule [government by one]
25. government by a few
26. straight writing
27. sharp tone [tone = *tonos*]
28. study of old life
29. all-imitator
30. [one speaking] many tongues
31. first witness
32. false name
33. love of wisdom
34. dry writing
35. beautiful writing

Exercise 2: Give opposites of:

1. heterodoxy [dox- opinion]
2. microcosm
3. allogamy
4. cacophony
5. allopathy
6. homgeneous
7. polyphone
8. monochrome
9. misology
10. calligraphy
11. omicron
12. paleocene

Exercise 3: take apart; define parts; explain [briefly] meaning of the whole

1. acromegaly
2. acropolis
3. allogamy
4. autoecious
5. isobar
6. bathymetry
7. etymography
8. eurybathic
9. brachylogy
10. gymnobiblism
11. heterology
12. hieroglyph [*gluphein* carve]
13. Holocene
14. homeopathy
15. hygroscope
16. idiolatry
17. isotope
18. pleistocene
19. kaleidoscope [*eidos* form, what is seen]
20. caceconomy
21. cenobiarch
22. megalomania
23. omicron
24. macron
25. monologue
26. myriapod
27. oligocene
28. orthoepy   [*epos* word]
29. paleontology   [*-ont-* being]
30. pantheon
31. platypus
32. polyphone
33. prototype
34. gymnosophist
35. theosophy
36. stenography
37. stereophonic
38. stereoscope
39. isotherme
40. trachea
41. xerophil
42. telemetry
43. polychromatic
44. gymnophilia
45. holograph
46. isosceles   [*skelos*, leg]
47. pliocene
48. megalomorph
49. monoecious [*oikos*]
50. orthoscope

Exercise 4 Make up or find five words using each of these:

1. autos
2. prōtos
3. megas
4. micros
5. macros
6. monos
7. polus
8. pseudes
9. tēle
10. palaios
11. neos
12. allos

Example: pas [bases *pan-*, *panto-*]:   pantomime, panacea, pantheon, pancreas, panoply, panegyric, pangenesis, pandemic, pandect, pandaemonium, panorama, pantograph, pantothenic acid, Pan-American, Pan-Hellenic

Exercise 5 [optional] Interesting words using new vocabulary. Choose 3 or 4 and find their origins and meanings:

1. elixir
2. sophomore
3. autarky
4. Jerome
5. hoi polloi
6. pancreas
7. panacea
8. minster [as in *Westminster*]
9. autacoid
10. Eurydice
11. idiot
12. place
13. panoply
14. panegyric
15. protocol
16. cholesterol
17. phylloxera
18. xerox
19. barium
20. coenurus
21. autochthonous [*chthon*, the earth]
22. cacoepy [*epos*, word]
23. oxymoron [*moros*, fool]
24. coenosarc [*sarx, sarc-* flesh]
25. etymon
26. pseudepigrapha
27. autopsy [*opsis* sight]
28. gymnosophist

Exercise 6   Give examples of:

1. acronyms
2. allegory
3. oxymoron
4. cacoepy
5. cacoethes
6. cenobium
7. homograph
8. homonyms
9. cacography
10. pseudonym

New words in the exercises

chthōn   *earth*
dikē   *justice*
epos   *word*
kolla   *glue*
kreas   *flesh, meat*
meros   *part*
mōros   *fool*
odous, odont—   *tooth*
sarx, sark—   *flesh*
skelos   *leg*
sperma, spermat—   *seed*
taphos   *tomb*
tonos   *tone, accent*

Use each of these word elements in an English word.

Check list

1. Greek adjectives: review; use each in a word
2. New words in lesson: learn interesting ones and use them in
sentences.

Supplement for chapter ten

Greek numbers

half	*hēmi-*
one	*hen-, en-*
first	*prōto-*
single	*mono-*
two	*di-, dy-*
second	*deutero-*
in two	*dicho-*
double	*diplo-*
three	*tri-*
four	*tetra-*
five	*pente-*
six	*hex-*
seven	*hepta-*
eight	*octo-*
nine	*ennea-*
ten	*deka-, deca-*
twenty	*icos-*
hundred	*hecato-*
thousand	*chili-, chilo-, kilo-*
number	*arithmo-*
angle	*gonia, -gon*
plane [seat]	*-hedron*
line	*-gram*
many	*poly-*
few	*oligo-*
and, plus	*kai*

1. Fill in Latin equivalents.
2. Tell how many:

triskaidekaphobia	dodecahedron
hexapolis	hemisphere
diplopia	chiliast
pentagon	ennead
triglyph	hemistich
monograph	kilometer
hexagram	Pentateuch
trilogy	distich
triptych	oligarchy
pentathlon	octohedron
decalogue	hecatomb
dichotomy	hexameter
tetrarchy	Deuteronomy
protagonist	deuteragonist
tritagonist	

Some interesting words derived from Greek numbers: diploma, hectare, enosis, dimity, hendiadys, hyphen, trapezoid, Pentecost, tetra, trivet

Numbers Game: ordinal/cardinal

Match cardinals with ordinals of the same rank and language: this game uses both Greek and Latin.

Proto-Geometric	quinquennium
Deuteronomy	sexpartite
tritagonist	biceps
primogeniture	enotic
secondguess	trilateral
tertiary	December
quartan fever	quadrivium
quintessential	duopsony
sextant	unitarian
decimal	triarchy

Words in Context

Polyglot waiters can tell us when the train starts in four or five languages. [1873]

This same *philosophy* is a good horse in the stable, but an arrant jade on a journey.

Oliver Goldsmith

Philologists who chase
A panting syllable through time and space,
Start it at home, and hunt it in the dark,
To Gaul, to Greece, and into Noah's ark.

Cowper

The *Philatelist* Royal
Was always too loyal
To say what he honestly
Thought of *Philately*

Robert Graves

Histories make men wise; poets, witty; the mathematics, subtle; natural *philosophy*, deep; moral, grave; *logic* and *rhetoric* able to contend.

Francis Bacon

Hardy became a sort of village *atheist* brooding and *blaspheming* over the village *idiot*.

G. K. Chesterton

123

Chapter Eleven: Greek suffixes

Noun and adjective forming suffixes

-ic, -tic   *pertaining to, having to do with*
        ethnic having to do with a people or nation

-ac   used instead of *-ic* if an *-i* immediately precedes
        cardiac having to do with the heart

-ics   [Greek, *-ika*] *things having to do with > art, science, study of* [used with a *singular* verb]
        acoustics study of sounds/things that are heard

[-ical   *-ic + -al*, from Latin *pertaining to, having the nature of*
        political pertaining to citizens/having to do with the relationship of citizens to the state [*polis*]

-oid   *resembling, like, shaped*
        android {thing that is} man-shaped

-ite   *one connected with, inhabitant of; a commercial product*
        sybarite an inhabitant of Sybaris > a person devoted to luxurious living; a hedonist
        lucite a clear {transparent} commercial product

-ism   *the belief in, profession or practice of*
        hylozoism belief in connection of life and matter

-ist   *one who believes in, professes, or practices, a follower of*
        dramatist one who makes plays

-ast   *one who does or practices, one who believes in*
        dicast one who does justice

-isk, -iscus   *small*
        asterisk a little star

-ia, -y   *act, state of* [abstract noun forming suffix]
        polity state of being a citizen: relation of citizens to the state

-sis   *act, state of*
        kenosis condition of being emptied

-m, -me, -ma   [base, *-mat-*] *result of*
        theorem result of observing
        theme result of setting

Exercise 1 Using vocabulary of previous lessons, make up words meaning:

1. one who studies causes
2. one who studies winds
3. human-like
4. one who studies [what is] worthy [i.e. value judgments]
5. one afflicted with a mad desire for books
6. having to do with many colors
7. having to do with time
8. things having to do with written records concerning the people [i.e. populations]
9. having to do with nations
10. things having to do with customs
11. earthlike
12. one having many marriages
13. fishlike
14. having to do with the universe
15. having to do with rings
16. stonelike
17. things having to do with measures
18. state of single marriage
19. act of measuring earth
20. one who studies stories
21. one who studies birds
22. having to do with the birth of mountains
23. things having to do with the healing of children
24. having to do with one's father's name
25. of the study of the soul
26. belief in many gods
27. of/having another form
28. of recent life
29. of beautiful writing
30. having solid voice
31. toothlike
32. of suffering [experience] from afar
33. things having to do with the law of the household

Exercise 2: Take apart and define:

1. chthonic
2. epic
3. oxytonic
4. orthodontist
5. necrosis
6. chiliast
7. android
8. misoneism
9. macrobiotic
10. kenosis
11. cryogenics
12. geopolitics
13. zodiac [< *zodiakos kuklos*] [< *zodion*, diminutive of <u>zoon</u>]
14. asterisk
15. gymnast

16. necrographist
17. axiologist
18. demotic
19. sophism
20. telepathy
21. monomaniac
22. typographical
23. prototypical
24. theism
25. telekinesis [< *kinein* move]

Exercise 3 make up words from these bases using as many of the new suffixes as you can:

1. mimos
2. axios
3. chroma, chromat-
4. ethos
5. cosmos
6. aster
7. schole
8. tupos
9. oikos
10. psuche
11. hupnos [sleep]

Example: **anthropos** [human being]: anthrop*oid*, philanthrop*ic*, philanthrop*ist*, misanthropy, anthropolog*ical*, anthropomorph*ism*, anthropopath*ism*, anthropogene*sis*

Vocabulary: go over these; learn any marked with an asterisk

* **agros** *field, land*
angos *vessel*
***anthos** *blossom, flower*
chēmeia [chemo-] *art of alloying metals >* chemicals, chemical
    reactions
chlōros *green*
chrusos *gold*
deinos [dino-] *terrible*
ēlektron *amber*
erēmos *lonely, desert*
gala, galakto- *milk*
hēlix, hēlico- *spiral*
* **hippos** *horse*
hoplon *armor*
hugiēs *healthy*
* **hulē** *material* as suffix -yl
* **hupnos** *sleep*
husteros *later, behind*
katharos *clean, pure*
keras *horn*
kolla *glue*
kuōn, kun- *dog*

magos   *enchanter, wizard*
mēchanē   *contrivance, machine*
mitos   *thread*
oura   *tail*
pelagos   *sea*
phrēn   [sometimes *fren-*]   *midriff, diaphragm, mind*
* phulē   *tribe*
* phullon   *leaf*
polemos   *war*
potamos   *river*
* rhētor   *orator*
rhodon   *rose*
* sauros   *lizard*
sklēros   *hard*
* sēma, semat-   *sign, signal*
stear   *fat*
toxon   *bow and arrows > arrow poison > poison*
zumē   *yeast*

Exercise 4

A.   Take these apart
  1.   colloid
  2.   agronomic
  3.   anthology
  4.   tyrannosaurus
  5.   intergalactic
  6.   phrenetic
  7.   sematic
  8.   hypnosis
  9.   hylozoism
 10.   hoplite
 11.   chemotherapy
 12.   chlorosis
 13.   helicoid
 14.   hipparch
 15.   cynophile
 16.   mitosis
 17.   polemics
 18.   eremite
 19.   rhetorical
 20.   panoply
 21.   catharsis
 22.   dinokeras
 23.   magic
 24.   phylum
 25.   sclerosis
 26.   chrysanthemum
 27.   electrotype
 28.   angiosperm
 29.   toxemia
 30.   stearic
 31.   phylogeny

B.   Make up words meaning:

   1.   terrible lizard
   2.   river horse
   3.   fear of dogs
   4.   passion for horses
   5.   tree rose
   6.   leaf green
   7.   poison-like
   8.   fish lizard
   9.   having to do with cleaning
  10.   state of flowering
  11.   study of vessels
  12.   leaflike

C.   Some interesting words derived from the new vocabulary

   1.   Hygeia
   2.   protocol
   3.   toxin
   4.   Mesopotamia
   5.   archipelago
   6.   alchemy
   7.   eohippus
   8.   hysteron proteron
   9.   helicopter
  10.   cynic
  11.   Philip
  12.   Phyllis

Check list for chapter eleven

1.   Learn all **suffixes**.

2.   Learn new **vocabulary**.

Make a chart of suffixes and use each in a word.

Medical Suffixes

-acousia/acusia, -acousis/acusis *hearing*
-agra *violent pain*
-algesia *excessive sensitivity to pain*
-algia *pain*
-aphia *touch*
-asthenia *loss of strength*
-auxe *enlargement*
-be *life, organism*
-blast *embryonic cell*
-cele *herniation*
-centesis *surgical puncture*
-ceros/cerus *horn [cf. corn-, Lat., horn]*
-clasis *a breaking up, dissolution*
-clastic *pertaining to dissolution*
-clysis *irrigation, washing*
-col *glue, jelly, gelatin*
-cyesis *pregnancy*
-dipsia *thirst*
-ectasia, -ectasis *dilation, stretching*
-ectomy *excision*
-edema *swelling*
-emesis *vomiting*
-emia, -hemia *blood condition*
-esthesia *sensation, feeling*
-genesis *formation, development*
-geustia, -geusia, -geusis *taste*
-iatrics, -iatry *healing, medical art*
-itis *inflammation*
-kinesia *movement*
-lepsy *seizure*
-lite, -lith *stone*
-lysis *destruction, breaking down*
-malacia *softening*
-mania *madness*
-megaly *enlargement*
-odia, -osmia *smell*
-odynia *pain*
-oma *tumor*
-oncus *tumor*
-opis, -opsis, -opsy *vision*
-orexia, -orexis *appetite*
-orrhagia *rapid discharge*
-orrhaphy *suture*
-orrhea *flow, discharge*
-orrhexis *rupture*
-osis *abnormal condition*
-osphresia, -osphresis *smell*
-ostomy *formation of a new opening*
-otomy *incision*
-pathy *disease*
-penia *deficiency*

-pepsia *digestion*
-pexy *fixation*
-phagia, -phagy *eating, swallowing*
-philia, -phily *love, affinity for*
-phobia *abnormal or morbid fear*
-phoria *feeling, bearing*
-phyma *swelling*
-plasia *formation, development*
-plasty *surgical repair, plastic surgery*
-plegia *stroke, paralysis*
-poiesis *formation, generation*
-ptosis *prolapse, sagging*
-schisis *splitting*
-sclerosis *hardening*
-sepsis *infection*
-spasm *twitching*
-stasis *controlling, checking, stopping*
-stat *device to check/stop*
-stenosis *stricture*
-therapy *treatment*
-tome *instrument to cut*
-tripsy *surgical crushing*
-trophy *development*
-uria *condition of urine*

What seems to be the problem?

1. anorexia
2. dyspepsia
3. cytopenia
4. anemia
5. diplopia
6. cephaloma
7. aerophagy
8. dactylospasm
9. cardiomegaly
10. odontalgia
11. podagra
12. neuromalacia
13. cephalalgia
14. megalomania
15. hemiplegia
16. hematuria
17. sclerosis
18. laryngalgia
19. hematocele
20. logorrhea
21. dysphoria
22. osteomalacia
23. cephalospasm
24. psychopathy
25. osteoma
26. osteoclasis
27. somatosmia
28. podosphresia

Body Parts

English	Greek	Latin
ankle	sphyron	tarsus
anus	proctos	anus
arm	brachion	brachium
beak, snout	rhynchos	rostrum
belly	gaster	venter
bladder	cystis	vesica
blood	haima, -at-	sanguis
body	soma, -at-	corpus
bone	osteon	os, oss-
brain	encephalos	cerebrum
breast	sternon, mastos	pectus, -or-; sternum, mamma
bristle	chaite	seta
cartilage	chondros	
cell	cytos	cella
cheek	pareia, genys	bucca
chest	stethos	
claw	chele, onyx	unguis
crest	lophos	crista
crown	stephanos	corona
digit	dactylos	digitus
ear	ous, -ot-	auris
egg	oon	ovum
eye	omma, ophthalmos	oculus
eyelash, -lid	blepharon	cilium
eyebrow	ophrys	supercilium
face	ops, opsis	facies
feather	pteron, ptilon	penna, pinna, pluma
flesh	creas, sarx	caro, carn-
foot	pous, pod-	pes, ped-
forehead	metopon	frons, front-
gland	aden	glans, gland-
hair	thrix, trich-	capillus, crinis, pilus
hand	cheir, chir-	manus
head	cephale	caput, capit-
heart	cardia	cor, cord-
heel	pterna	talus, calx
hip	ischion, hypokolion	coxa
horn	keras, -at-	cornu
jaw	gnathos, genys	maxilla
joint	arthron	artus, articulus
kidney	nephros	renes
knee	gonu	genu
knuckle	condulos	
leg	skelos	crus, crur-
lip	cheilos	labium, labrum
liver	hepar, hepat-	jecur, jecor-
lung	pneumon	pulmo, pulmon-
membrane	hymen	membrana
mouth	stoma, -at-	os, or-
mucus	blenna, myxa	
muscle	mys, myo-	

neck	auchen, dere, trachelos	cervix, -ic-, collum
nose	rhis, rhin-	nares, nasus
rib	pleura, skelis	costa
scale	lepis, -id-	squama
shoulder	omos	scapula
skin	derma, -at-	cutis
skull	cranion	
sperm	sperma	semen, -in-
stomach	gaster	venter
tail	oura, cercos	cauda
thigh	ischion	femur, -or-
thorax	thorax	
throat	pharynx, laimos	gula, guttur
tissue	istos	tela
tongue	glossa	lingua
tooth	odous, odont-	dens, dent-
vein	phleps, phleb-	vena
windpipe	tracheia, bronchos	
wing	pteron	ala
wrist	carpos	carpus

Exercises

1. A person who is *callisphyrous* has beautiful _____.
2. The *metatarsal* bones are behind the _____ [five bones between the tarsus and the toes, forming the instep].
3. *Aproctous* insects have no _____.
4. A *rhyncocephalian* has a _____ on its head.
5. *Binoculars* are for both _____.
6. The *rostrum* in the Roman forum was so called because it was decorated with the _____ of captured ships.
7. A *gastric* ulcer is an open sore in the _____.
8. *Cystitis* is an inflammation of the _____.
9. A *hypochodriac* experiences pain from imaginary illnesses arising from the region under the _____ of the breastbone [the seat of melancholy].
10. A *hemorrhage* is a copious discharge of _____.
11. *Encephalitis* is inflammation of the _____.
12. A *brachiopod* has a pair of _____like tentacled structures on either side of its mouth.
13. *Somatogenic* compensations arise within the _____ in response to the environment.
14. A *pectoral* is worn over the _____.
15. *Osteomyelitis* is an inflammation of the _____ marrow.
16. A *pterodactyl* is an extinct flying reptile, called wing-_____.
17. A *rostrate biped* has a pair of _____ and a _____.
18. A *cristate* helmet is _____.
19. A *supercilious* person often raises his/her _____ disdainfully.
20. *Genyplasty* is plastic surgery on the _____.
21. A *pterosaur* is a _____ lizard.
22. The *oculomotor* nerve controls the muscles of the _____.
23. The *ootheca* is the _____case of certain insects.

133

24. A *setaceous quadruped* has _____ and four _____.
25. *Oology* is that branch of ornithology that deals with birds' _____.
26. A *sarcophagus* is a stone coffin; its name means _____ - eating.
27. *Surgeon* is derived from Greek <u>cheirurgus</u> which means working with the _____.
28. *Carnal* sin is of the _____.
29. *Metopic* wrinkles are creases on the _____.
30. A *capillary* resembles a _____.
31. A *trichome* is a _____like growth.
32. A *depilatory* removes _____.
33. An *adenectomy* is the surgical removal of a _____.
34. *Myogenic* growths arise from the _____ tissue.
35. An *isosceles* triangle has two equal _____.
36. An abscess of the *myocardium* would affect the _____ tissue around the _____.
37. A *cheirosopher* is skilled in the _____.
38. The Rev. Mr. John Newton named his collected letters *Cardio- phonia*, or "Utterances from the _____."
39. A *myogram* is a _____ of _____ contractions and re- laxations.
40. A *cardiognost* is one who knows the _____: "As if they were cardiognosts and fully versed in his intentions."
41. A *chiropodist* treats diseases of the _____ and _____.
42. *Nephrolithotomy* is the removal of a _____ from the _____.
43. *Keratin* is a substance found in the _____.
44. *Renal calculi* are _____ _____.
45. *Gnathopods* are Crustaceans that have _____-_____.
46. *Nephrorrhaphy* is the operation of fixing a movable _____ by _____.
47. To *chirotonize* is to elect by show of _____.
48. The *condyloid* process is like a _____.
49. *Arthrology* is a) a treatise on _____ or b) the hand signs of the deaf and mute.
50. *Pneumonoconiosis* is a disease of the _____ caused by the inhalation of dust.
51. A *chilocace* is a canker of the _____.
52. *Hymenoptera* is a large order of insects having four _____ _____.
53. *Maxillary* glands are in the region of the _____.
54. A *cervix* is any _____-shaped anatomical structure.
55. *Squamous* creatures are covered with _____.
56. The *cuticle* is the strip of hardened _____ at the base of the finger- or toenail.   In Botany, it is the layer of *cutin* [a waxlike, water-repellant material present in some plant cells] covering the *epidermis* [or _____ _____ layer] of plants.
57. The *calcaneus* is the quadrangular bone at the back of the tarsus and is also called the _____ bone.
58. An *omophore* bears a great weight of his _____.
59. *Blennorrhea* is discharge of _____.
60. A *blenny* is a small marine fish named for the _____ coat- ing on its scales.
61. To *genuflect* is to bend the _____.
62. Another name for *femur* is the _____ bone.

63. *Phlebotomy* is the practice of cutting open a _____ to let the blood flow [also called *bleeding*].
64. *Ischiatic* means pertaining to the _____.
65. A *myxoma* is a benign tumor composed of connective tissue and _____ elements.
66. The *metacarpus* is behind the _____.
67. *Coxalgia* is a _____ in the _____.
68. A *costate* leaf has _____.
69. "A *caudate* variety of the human species" would have a _____.
70. A *coda* is the conclusion [or _____] of a movement.
71. A *guttural* sound is produced in the _____.
72. *Alate* animals have _____.
73. *Craniotabes* is a wasting of the _____ bone.
74. The *mastodon* is named _____-_____ because of the nipple-like protuberances on its _____.
75. A *histoblast* is the primary element of a _____.
76. *Bronchophony* is the sound of the voice heard in the _____ by means of a stethoscope.
77. *Narial* hairs grow in the _____.
78. A *pachyderm* has a thick _____.
79. A *rhapsode* is a _____ of songs.
80. The *crural* nerve is in the _____.
81. The *omoplate* is the _____ or in Latin the _____.
82. A *scapular* is worn about the _____.
83. *Phlebostenosis* is abnormal _____ of the _____.
84. *Histophyly* is the history of _____ within the limits of a particular tribe [*phyle*] of organisms.
85. *Apterous* aphids have ____ _____.

Chapter Twelve: Greek Prefixes

* a- [an- before a vowel] *not, un-, -less*

amphi- *both, on both sides, around, about*

* ana- [an- before a vowel] *up, back, again*

anti- *instead, against, in opposition to*

* apo, ap- *from, away from, off, utterly, completely, lack of*

* dia-, di- *through, across, over, assunder*

dys- [Greek, *dus-*] *ill, un-, mis-, difficult, bad*

* ec-, ex [Greek, *ek-*] *out, from, off*

ecto- [Greek, *ekto-*] *on the outside*

* en-, em- *in*

enantio- [*en- + anti-*] *opposite*

endo- *within, inside, internal*

eso- *inward, within*

exo- *outward, external*

* epi-, ep- *upon, over, at, near*

* eu-, ev- *well, good*

* cata-, cat- [Greek, *kata*] *down, against, completely [opp. ana-]*

* meta-, met- *among, between, change, behind, later*

palin-, pali- *back, again*

* para-, par- *beside, beyond, near, incorrectly, like*

* peri- *around, about*

* pro- *before, forward, for*

pros- *to, toward, besides, in front*

* syn-, sym-, sys- [Greek, *sun*] *with, together*

* hyper- [Greek, *huper*] *above, beyond, exceedingly*

* hypo-, hyp- [Greek, *hupo*] *under*

Exercise 1 Take apart and define parts:

1. symbiosis
2. enantiobiosis
3. catholic
4. palinode [ode, song]
5. parody
6. antagonist [agon, struggle, contest]
7. empathy
8. sympathy
9. analgesic
10. parallel [allelon, each other]
11. amphibian
12. euthanasia [thanatos, death]
13. energetic
14. synergy
15. ephemeral [hemera, day]
16. Eucharistic [charis, grace, thanks]
17. perimeter
18. anarchist
19. paragraph
20. dialogue
21. metamorhosis
22. analogy
23. endomorph
24. metempsychosis
25. encyclical
26. pseudepigrapha
27. evangelical
28. epigraphy
29. endemic

Using the base of hodos, *road, way*

30. anode
31. cathode
32. method
33. period
34. episode
35. exodos
36. eisodos
37. parodos
38. synod
39. odograph
40. odometer

Optional exercise: Choose one prefix and find as many words as you can using it. Make sure they are all legitimate.
Example: **kata-:** catholic, cathode, cathedral, cathexis, cation, catheter, catechism, catechumen, category, catastrophe, catalogue, catabolic, catachresis, catadromous, catalepsy, catalyst.
But *not:* catalpa [from Creek, not Greek], catamaran [from Tamil], catamount ["cat of the mountains"], catalo [cattle + buffalo], catenary [< Latin catena, chain], catamite [< Ganymede]

Exercise 2:   Word words [from *onoma*, using element -onym]: take
apart and explain parts.   Give an example of each or use it in a
sentence.

1.   anonymous
2.   eponymous
3.   paronymous
4.   metonymy
5.   synonym
6.   antonym
7.   homonym
8.   acronym
9.   pseudonymous
10. euonymous

Exercise 3   Make up compounds from these bases,   using the   new
prefixes:

1.   logos
2.   kuklos
3.   metron
4.   ergon
5.   pathos
6.   demos
7.   gram-, -graph
8.   derma [skin]

Exercise 4:   Make up words meaning:

1.   instrument for looking around
2.   absence of feeling
3.   without color
4.   one bringing a good message
5.   upon the people
6.   having to do with writing on stones
7.   good sound
8.   measure through
9.   at the same time [timed with]
10. of change in shape

Exercise 5:   Review of prefixes and suffixes.   Fill in one word
using the same prefix as the word given and one word using the
same suffix:

    apathetic   atheist   *archaeologist*
                             amphiarthrosis [*arthron* joint]
                             anarchy
                             analytic [*luein* loosen]
                             antiphonal
                             aposiopesis [*siope* silence]
                             diagnostics [*gno-* perceive]
                             dysteleological
                             ecdysiast [*ekduein* take off]
                             ectoderm
                             encephalitis

139

```
enantiomorph
endocrinology [krinein separate]
esoterism [-ter- more]
exodontia
epidermoid
eupatrid [-id son of]
catalogue
metaphysics [physis nature]
palindrome [dromos a running]
paradigmatic [dig- < deik- show]
periodical
problem [bal-, ble- throw]
prosthesis [the- put]
symmetry
hyperopia [opia eye condition]
hypochondriac [chondros cartilage]
```

Check list

Know all Greek prefixes
Make a chart using each prefix in a word

Words in Context

Nowadays his thought was rarely abstract. The abstract stabbed—it was too personal. But he kept by him the bitter *homonym*, the notion of Principle embodied in a Principal, his own comfortless comical *theory*—ha!—of flawed incarnation. And he held also to another secret pun, delivered by himself to himself for the sole consequence of a nasty cackle: the Fleg of the Edmond Fleg School, what was it short for? Answer: *Phlegmatic*. And what else? Answer: *Phlegethon*, the river of fire that runs through Hell.

                                        Cynthia Ozick

Human history becomes more and more a race between education and *catastrophe*.

                                        H. G. Wells

The speaking in perpetual *hyperbole* is comely in nothing but in love.

                                        Francis Bacon

Supplement for lesson twelve

Greek and Latin prefixes compared; English cognates included

Greek	Latin	English cognate
a-, an- [not]	ne-, in-	no, none, nay, naught
amphi- [around]	ambi-	by, be-
ana- [on]		a- [as in aloft], on-
anti- [against]	ante- [in front]	un-, along, end
apo- [off, away]	ab-	of, off, ebb, after
dia- [through]		
dys- [bad]	= mis- [not cognate]	
ec-, ex- [out]	ex-, extra-, extro-	

en- [in]
  endo-, eso-,
  eis- [into]
	in-, intro, intra,
	  inter, intus
		in, and

epi- [near]	ob- [to, against]	
eu- [well]		
cata- [down]	cf. catulus [young puppy < something thrown down]	
meta- [between]		cf. midwife

para-, peri-,
  pro-, pros-
  [basic meaning:
  forward]
	per-, pro-, prae
	  cf. primus
		far, for, fore-, first

syn- [with]	cf. simul, semper	
hyper- [over]	super-, supra-	over

hypo- [under, up
  from under]
  cf. hypso-
	sub-, subter-
	  cf. supinus
		up, above, open; evil

Latin: *ad-*/ English *at*
Greek: *koinos*/ Latin *com-*
Latin: *de-*/English *to, too*
Greek: *zeugma*/ Latin *juxta-*/ English *yoke*
Latin: *se-, sine-*/ English *asunder*
Latin: *trans-*/ English *through, thorough, nostril*

141

Word Game: Pitfalls

Which are from Greek?

                parachute
                catalpa
                anaconda
                anticipate
                aport
                enmity
                ephah
                euchre
                meticulous
                palisade
                periwinkle
                proa
                syllabub
                hyson

Some interesting words using the new Greek prefixes: [Optional]
Choose one and explain it and find an example or picture.

                palimpsest
                aposiopesis
                apophthegm
                aphorism
                peristyle
                prostyle
                Peripatetic
                prosopopoeia
                catapult
                syllogism
                apostrophe
                synecdoche
                anaphora
                periodic style
                peripateia
                hysteron proteron
                hyperbole
                parataxis
                hypotactic
                anapest
                asyndeton
                epithalamium
                antistrophe
                anagnorisis

Distinguish:
                epigraph   metaphor
                epitaph   metonymy
                epigram   allegory
                epithet   simile
                epitome
                epode

                        142

Chapter Thirteen: Greek Verbs

Study the verb stems and meanings in the list below.   The Greek
present infinitive is given in brackets.

ag- [agein] *lead, bring*
    -agogue [from -*agogos*] "one leading" > **pedagogue**
    or [from -*agoge*] "a leading, gathering" > **synagogue**

aesth-, esth- [aisthanesthai] *feel, perceive*

acou, acu- [akouein] *hear*

ba-, be- [bainein] *go, step, walk*

ball-, ble-, bol- [ballein] *throw*

chor- [chōrein] *move*
    -chore indicates a plant distributed by a specific agency >
    anemochore

do- [didonai] *give*

doc-, dog-, dox- [dokein] *seem, think*
    doxa *opinion, praise, reputation*

drom- [dramein] *run*

dra- [dran] *do, act, perform*

dyn- [dunasthai] *be able, be powerful*
    dunamis *power*

hek-, hex-, sche-, och-, -uch- [echein] *have, hold*

-ont-, -ous- [einai] *be* [root, -es]

i- [ienai] *go*

gno- [gignōskein] *know*

glyph- [gluphein] *carve*

graph-, gram- [graphein] *draw, write*

sta-, ste- [histanai] *stand*

cle- [kalein] *call*

cin-, kin- [kinein] *move*

clin- [klinein] *bend, make to slope*

cop-, com- [koptein] *cut*

crin-, cri- [krinein] *separate, judge, decide*

crypt-, cryp- [kruptein] *hide*

lab-, lēp-, lem- [lambanein] *take, seize*

leg-, lex-, lect-, log- [legein] *gather, say*

ly- [luein] *loose, break, destroy*

math- [manthanein] *learn*

nem-, nom- [nemein, cf. *nomos*] *assign, allot*

pau-, -pose (with meaning influenced by Latin *ponere*) [pauein]
    cease, stop

phag- [phagein] *eat*
    -phage "one who/that which eats"
    -phagous "eating"
    -phagy "the habit or tendency to eat"

phain-, phen-, phan- [phainein] *show, cause to appear; appear*

pha-, phe- [phanai] *say, speak* (pheme a *saying*)

pher-, phor- [pherein] *bear, carry*

phy- [phuein] *make to grow; grow, be by nature*

poie-, poe- [poiein] *make, do*

pol- [pōlein] *sell*

prag-, prak-, prac- [prattein] *do*

rhe(u)-, rhy-, rho- [rhein] *flow*

schiz-, schis- [schizein] *split*

scop-, skop-, scep-, skep- [scōpein] *examine, look at*

stol-, stal-, stl- [stellein] *send, make ready*

tak-, tac-, tax- [tattein] *arrange, assign, assess*

tme-, tom- [temnein] *cut*

troph- [trephein] *feed, nourish*

trop(h)- [trepein] *turn*

ten-, ta-, ton- [teinein] *stretch out, strain*

the- [tithenai] *put, place*

Exercise 1: Find common verb stem in each group; take apart and explain meaning of whole.

1. demagogue, pedagogue
2. aesthetic, anesthesia
3. acoustics, pseudacusis
4. acrobat, diabetes
5. problem, metabolism
6. anemochore, anchorite
7. anecdote, apodosis
8. dogmatic, heterodox
9. dromedary, hippodrome
10. dramatic, drastic
11. dynasty, dynamite
12. cachexia, entelechy
13. ion, cation
14. ontological, paleontology
15. agnosticism, diagnosis
16. hieroglyphic, petroglyph
17. seismograph, diagram [seismos, *earthquake*]
18. ecstatic, iconostasis
19. paraclete, ecclesiastical
20. cinema, hyperkinetic
21. enclitic, climate
22. pericope, syncope
23. critic, hypocrisy
24. apocryphal, cryptogram
25. dilemma, epilepsy
26. eclectic, prologue
27. dyslexia, catalogue
28. psychoanalytic, paralysis
29. polymath, mathematics
30. nomad, nemesis
31. pause, menapause [men- *month*]
32. sarcophagus, papyrophagy
33. epiphany, phenomenon, diaphanous
34. prophesy, dysphasia
35. euphoria, anaphora
36. physics, neophyte
37. onomatopoetic, poem
38. bibliopole, monopoly
39. impractical, pragmatic
40. diarrhoea, logorrhoea, rheum
41. schismatic, schizogenesis
42. episcopal, telescope
43. epistle, apostolic
44. catastrophic, antistrophe
45. syntax, paratactic
46. atomic, dichotomy [dicha- *in two*]
47. atrophy, entrophic
48. heliotrope, tropic
49. monotone, hypotenuse [-use is the participial ending, =-*ing*]
50. parenthetical, metathesis, anathema

145

Exercise 2:   make up words meaning

1. tending to go down
2. result of throwing in
3. thing given against
4. of right opinion
5. instrument for measuring power
6. running up
7. a knowing before
8. far writing
9. act of standing away
10. act of calling upon
11. act of moving from afar
12. tending to judge under
13. book seller
14. a breaking up/down/through
15. fish, fowl, fire, flower, and foreigner eaters
16. study of things beyond nature
17. one who makes
18. seller of paper, of fish, of air
19. a turning away
20. a putting under/against/together

Some interesting words from the new Greek verbs:

agein   strategy
ballein   devil, parable, parliament
echein   eunuch, hectic
graphein   glamor, prolegomenon, hapax legomenon
koptein   comma
lambanein   narcolepsy, nympholepsy
poiein   poetaster
pherein   paraphernalia   [pherne *dowry*, that which is brought]
mathein   chrestomathy
skōpein   bishop
tithenai   boutique, bodega
prattein   barter
phainein   sycophant, phenomenon [-men- is a participial ending,
    also seen in prolegomenon, ecumenical]
phanai   blame, blasphemy
kruptein   grotto, grotesque

Exercise 3:   give examples of

1. paradox
2. hyperbole
3. palindrome
4. anagram
5. protasis
6. euphemism
7. metaphor
8. boustrophedon ["as the ox turns"]
9. tmesis
10. epithet

Exercise 4 review of verbs

A.   Match with meaning of base verb;   fill in one additional
English word using the same base.

_x_	apocryphal	1. know	crypt
___	mystagogue	2. go [2]	
___	esthete	3. run	
___	discobolus	4. be	
___	zoochore	5. have	
___	antidote	6. do	
___	doxology	7. lead	
___	catadromous	8. throw	
___	melodramatic	9. seem	
___	dynamic	10. give	
___	epoch	11. move	
___	cation	12. hear	
___	ontic	13. be able	
___	gnostic	14. feel	
___	acoustic	x. hide	
___	basis		

___	anaglyph	1. stop
___	program	2. learn
___	thermostat	3. gather
___	kinesthesia	4. hide
___	epiclesis	5. cut
___	proclitic	6. call
___	apocope	7. stand
___	endocrine	8. carve
___	cryptic	9. move
___	epilepsy	10. lean
___	analects	11. separate, judge
___	catalyst	12. take
___	monomath	13. loosen
___	anomy	14. write
___	diapause	15. assign

___	anthropophage	1. put
___	phantasmogoria	2. sell
___	prophesy	3. eat
___	dysphoria	4. cut
___	physics	5. flow
___	pharmacopoeia	6. seem, appear
___	oenopole	7. arrange
___	catarrh	8. make
___	schismatic	9. speak
___	epistolary	10. turn
___	apostrophe	11. grow
___	hypotactic	12. carry
___	nephrolithectomy	13. send
___	prosthesis	14. split

B. Match words from same verb and give meaning of verb base:

___ dialect   1. pericope
___ schism   2. emblematic
___ graphite   3. homoiousian
___ system   4. epigram
___ diacritical   5. poetry
___ dilemma   6. anabatic
___ dose   7. phantom
___ paradoxical   8. dogmatic
___ symbolic   9. criterion
___ basis   10. schizogenesis
___ stratagem   11. apostasy
___ ontological   12. synagogue
___ comma   13. dyslexia
___ mythopoeic   14. astrolabe
___ phenomenology   15. anecdotal

Word Game: which does not belong

demagogue   strategic   pedagogy   ago
acoustics   pseudacusis   acute
anabasis   stylobate   bass   acrobat
devil   ballistics   metabolic   Bolshevik
dos-a-dos   dose   antidote   anecdote
dramaturgy   dromedary   palindrome   hippodrome
hectic   hex   eunuch   cachexia
gnostic   genesis   prognosis   gnomic
graffiti   graminivorous   grammar   telegraph
cinerous   cinema   kinetic   telekinetic
criticaster   crinate   criterion   crisis
lyceum   lysis   catalyst   paralytic
polyandry   monopoly   oligopoly   oenopole
Prakrit   practical   pragmatic   praxis
thesis   thematic   parenthetical   theanthropism
epistle   apostolic   constellation   systalic

Check list for lesson 13

Learn Greek verb stems
Review prefixes and suffixes

Supplement to lesson thirteen: Some Greek and Latin verb formations compared:

dialysis	dissolution
hypostasis	substance
tmesis	caesura
synthesis	composition
anaesthetic	insensitive
acoustic	auditory
problem	project
dynast	potentate
syndrome	concourse
cachexia	disability
ontic	essential
diagram	transcript, description
ecclesiastic	evocative
pericope	circumcision
periphrasis	circumlocution
strophe	verse
apostle	missionary
episcopal	supervisory
epigraphic	inscriptional
erotic	amatory, amorous

Add to this list as a review of Greek and Latin elements of word formation.

Words in Context

...a falseness in all our impressions of external things which I would generally call the "*pathetic* fallacy"

Ruskin

Never make a defence of *apology* before you be accused.

Charles I

Poetry is not the proper *antithesis* to prose, but to science. Poetry is opposed to science, and prose to metre.

Coleridge

The excitement of being in Paris produced a sudden wild *euphoria*, the more intense by its contrast with the despairing lassitude in which she had recently been plunged.

Iris Murdoch

...he saw at last, with horrified wide-open eyes, the futility of philosophy. *Metaphysics* and the human sciences are made impossible by the penetration of morality into the moment to moment conduct of ordinary life.... This is what Rozanov distantly glimpsed when he was picking away at questions of good and evil, and he knew it made nonsense of all his *sophisms*.

Iris Murdoch

If you are anxious for to shine in the high *aesthetic* line...

W. S. Gilbert

Verbum sapienti: A note to the student

```
S_S_____N *
```

```
_____
I        I
I
I
I
I
I
```

Students of etymology derive many academic benefits
and we hope some fun as well. With words a foot &
a half long * you can gleefully garrotte your pals
during dull meetings, improve your trivial pursuit,
beat your profs at the dictionary game.
With *logomania* you need never be bored.

The Dictionary Game

Equipment: A big dictionary; scrap paper; one pencil for each
    player

How to play: The player who is *it* finds an obscure [and if
possible amusing] word in the Big Dictionary.   He/she announces
and spells the word for the other players who write it down on
their pieces of scrap paper.   If any player knows the word, that
word is disqualified. The player with the dictionary then writes
down the dictionary definition while each other player writes
down a definition of his/her own invention, aiming at the
greatest absurdity within the limits of dictionary diction.   *It*
then collects the definitions and reads them to the other players
who vote for the definition of their choice. Play continues.

Players receive points for votes for their false definitions. The
player who is *it* receives a point for each vote for a wrong definition.

> *I said it in Hebrew--I said it in Dutch--*
> *I said it in German and Greek;*
> *But I wholly forgot (and it vexes me much)*
> *That English is what you speak!*
>
>   Lewis Carroll

APPENDIX

Suffixes from Latin

-acious [6] < -ax, -ac- "tending to" forms adjectives from the present base of verbs

-al [2] < -alis "of, pertaining to" forms adjectives from noun bases

-alia, -ilia [2] < neuter plural of -alis, -ilis "things having to do with" forms plural nouns from adjectives in ilis/alis

-ance, -ence [6] < -antia, -entia "act, state, condition of..." forms nouns from present participles

-ane, -an [2] < -anus "of, pertaining to" forms adjectives from noun bases

-ant, -ent [6] < -ans, -ant-/-ens, -ent "-ing" present participle, forms adjectives [and nouns] from present base of verbs

-ar, -ary [2] < -aris "of, pertaining to" forms adjectives from noun bases

-ary, -arious [2] < -arius "of, pertaining to" forms adjectives from noun bases

-ary [2] < -arius masculine form "a person concerned with" forms nouns from adjectives in -arius

-ary, -arium [2] < -arium neuter form "a place for/of" forms nouns from adjectives in -arius

-ate [3] < -atus "office of" forms nouns from noun [or adjective] bases

-ate [2] "possessing" forms adjectives from noun bases

-ate [4] < -are, -atum "cause, make, use" forms verbs from noun bases

-at[e], -it[e] [7] forms verbs from ppp base of verbs: keep doing, do intensively [frequentative verbs]

-ble [-able, -ible] [6] < -bilis "able to be, able to" forms adjectives from either verb base

-ble [6] < -bulum, -bula "instrument or place for" forms nouns from the present base of verbs

-cide [4] < -cida "one who kills"; < -cidium "the killing of" forms nouns

-cle, -culum [6] < -*culum* "place or instrument for" forms nouns from the present base of verbs

-ence, see -ance

-ent, see -ant

-eous [2] <-*eus* "of, pertaining to" forms adjectives from noun bases

-ernal [2] < -*ernus* "of, pertaining to" forms adjectives from noun bases

-fer [4] <*ferre* "that which bears" forms nouns

-ferous [4] < *ferre* "bearing" forms adjectives

-fic [4] < *facere* "making, causing" forms adjectives

-fy [4] < *facere* "to make, cause" forms verbs

-ic [2] < -*icus* "of, pertaining to" forms adjectives from noun bases

-ice [3] < -*itia* "quality, state, condition, or character of being" forms nouns from adjective bases

-id [6] < -*idus* "tending to, of a quality" forms adjectives from the present base of verbs

-il, -ile [2] < -*ilis* "of, pertaining to" forms adjectives from noun bases

-ile [6] < -*ilis* "able to be" forms adjectives from the present base of verbs

-ine [2] < -*inus* "of, pertaining to" forms adjectives from noun bases

-ion [6, 7] < -*io*,-*ion*- "act, state, or result" forms nouns from ppp [and present] verb bases

-ity, -ety, -ty [3] < -*tas* "quality, state, condition or character of being" forms nouns from adjective [and noun] bases

-itude [3] < -*itudo*, -*itudin*- "state, quality, condition or character of being" forms nouns from adjective bases

-ive [7] < -*ivus* "tending to, having the quality of" forms adjectives from the ppp base of verbs

-lent [-olent, -ilent, -ulent] [2] < -*lentus* "full of, disposed to" forms adjectives from noun bases

-men [6] < -*men*, -*min*- "result, means of" forms nouns from

152

present base of verbs

-ment [6] < -*mentum* "result, means of" forms nouns from present base of verbs

-mony [3] < -*monium*, -*monia* "quality, state, condition, or character of being" forms nouns from adjective bases

-nal [2] < -*nus* + -al "of, pertaining to" forms adjectives from Latin adjectives in -*nus* [formed from noun bases]

-nd [6] < -*ndus* "that must be" forms gerundives from the present base of Latin verbs [nouns or adjectives in English]

-or [6] < -*or* "act, state, or result of" forms nouns from the present base of verbs

-or [7] < -*or* "one who, that which" forms nouns from the ppp base of verbs

-orious, -ory [7] < -*orius* "tending to, pertaining to" forms adjectives from the ppp base of verbs

-ose, -ous [2] < -*osus* "full of, having, tending to be" forms adjectives from noun bases

-ous [1] < -*us* forms English adjectives from Latin adjectives

-tic [2] < -*ticus* "of, pertaining to" forms adjectives from noun bases

-tude, see -itude

-ty, see -ity

-ulous [6] < -*ulus* "tending to" forms adjectives from present base of verbs

-uous [6] < -*uus* "tending to" forms adjectives from present base of verbs

-ure [7] < -*ura* "the act or result of" forms nouns from ppp base of verbs

-urnal [2] < -*urnus* + -al "of, pertaining to" forms adjectives from noun bases

-y [3] < -*ia* "quality, state, condition, or character of being" forms nouns from adjective bases

-y [3] < -*ium* "act, office, place, or position" forms nouns from noun bases

-y [6] < -*ium* "act, state, instrument, or result" forms nouns from prsent bases of verbs

A

acer, acr- (1) [3]	sharp, keen
aequus [equi-] (2)	even, *equal*
aevum [ev-] [3]	age
ager, agr- (1)	field
agere, actum [4]	do, drive, lead
ala (1)	wing
albus	white
alere, altum [6]	grow
alienus (4)	belonging to another
alter	other
altus (1)[3]	high, deep
amare	love
ambulare (2)	walk, go
amicus (3)	friend
amoenus [amen-]	pleasant
amplus [1]	large, spacious
ancilla	maidservant, handmaiden
anima [1]	breath
animus [1]	spirit
annus [2] [-enn-]	year
antiquus [1]	old
aperire, apertum [7]	open
apis (pl. apes) (4)	bee
aptus [3]	fitted to
aqua (1), [2]	water
aquila (1)	eagle
arbiter	witness, judge
arca (1)	chest
arcus	bow
ardēre, arsum (6)	burn
ars, art-	skill, craft
artus (3)	joint
asper	rough, bitter, harsh
atavus (4)	great-great-great-grandfather, ancestor
audēre	dare
audire, auditum (4)[6]	hear
augēre, auctum [6]	increase
augur (3)	soothsayer
aura	breeze
auris, aur- [3]	ear
auxilium	aid
avarus (3)	greedy
avis (pl. aves) (4)	bird
avus (4)	grandfather

B

baca, bacca (4)	berry
beatus [3]	happy, blessed
bellum	war
bellus	pretty, handsome

155

bene [1]	well
bi-, bin-, bis- (2)	two, by twos, twice
bibere (6)	drink
bonus [1]	good
bos, bov-	ox, bull, cow
brevis [1]	short

C

cadere, casum [4]	fall [-cid-, -cas-]
caedere, caesum [4]	cut, kill [-cid-, -cis-]
caelum	sky
calēre (6)	be warm
calumnia (1)	false accusation
calx, calc- (3)	pebble
campus	open field
candēre [6]	shine, be white
canere, cantum (4) [5]	sing
canis, can(i)- (2)	dog
capere, captum {-io} [4]	take, seize [-cipi-, -cept-; -ceive]
capsa (1)	box
caput, capit- [2]	head
carcer (5)	prison
cardo, cardin- (2)	hinge
caro, carn- [2]	flesh
castra (3)	camp
castus (6)	pure, chaste
causa [1]	cause, reason
cavus [3]	hollow
cedere, cessum [4]	go, yield
cella (3)	storeroom
centum (2)	hundred
cerebrum (3)	head, brain
censēre, censum [7]	assess, rate, estimate
cernere, cretum [5]	sift
civis, civ(i)- [2]	citizen
clamare, clamatum [4]	shout [claim]
clarus [1]	bright, *clear*
classis (3)	fleet
claudere, clausum [4]	shut [-clud-, -clus-; -close]
clavis (3)	key
clinare, clinatum	turn, bend
codex, codic- (3)	tree trunk, book
colere, cultum [7]	till, honor, dwell
comis	nice, courteous
condere, conditum [5]	build, store, hide
copia [2]	abundance, supplies
cor, cordi- (2)	heart
corium (5)	hide, skin
cornu (2)	horn
corona (3)	crown
corpus, corpor-, n. [1]	body
creare, creatum [6]	create
credere, creditum [7]	believe

crescere, cretum (6)	grow [inchoative of *creare*]
crux, cruc(i)- (4)	cross
culpa (5)	fault
currere, cursum (4) [5]	run
cutis (3)	skin

D

dare, datum [4]	give [-dere, -dit-]
debēre, debitum	owe
decem (2)	ten
dens, dent- (5)	tooth
deus, de- (4)	god, God
dexter	right hand
dicere, dictum (4) [5]	say
dies, di- [2]	day
difficilis [1]	hard
dignus [1]	worthy
diluvium	flood
discipulus (3)	pupil, *disciple*
divus [1]	of a god, *divine*
docēre, doctum [6]	teach
dolēre, dolitum	be in pain, grieve
dominus (4)	master < *domus*
domus [domes-] [1]	home, house
donum (4)	gift
dorsum	back
dubius (1)	doubtful
ducere, ductum [4]	lead
duo (2)	two

E

effetus (1)	worn out by child-bearing
emere, emptum (4) [5]	buy
equi- (2) see *aequus*	
equus	horse
errare, erratum [4]	go astray
esse, futurum [6]	be
experiri, expertum (6)	try, test

F

facilis [1]	easy
facere, factum {-io} [4]	do, make [-fici-, -fect-]
fama	talk, rumor
fanum [2]	temple
fari, fatum [6]	speak
fatēri, fassum	acknowledge [-fit-,-fess-]
fatum [1]	the thing said, fate
fatuus [3]	silly, foolish

fecundus	fertile
felix, felic–	happy
femina	woman
–fendere, –fensum [7]	strike, hurt
ferre [fer–], latum [4]	bear, carry
ferus (1)	wild
fervēre [6]	boil
fidere [6]	trust, rely on
findere, fissum [7]	split
fingere, fictum [7]	form
finis [1]	end
flamma (4)	torch, fire, *flame*
flectere, flexum [5]	bend
flos, flor–	flower
fluere, fluxum [6]	flow
fluctus (4)	wave
focus [1]	hearth
forma [3]	shape, beauty
fortis [3]	strong, brave
forum (1)	public place, market
frangere [frag–], fractum [6]	break
frater, fratr(i) (4)	brother
frustra (4)	in vain
fugere [–io], fugitum [7]	flee
fumus (6)	smoke, steam
fundere, fusum [5]	pour
fundus (1)	bottom, landed property
fungi, functum [7]	perform
funus, funer– [2]	death, rites for the dead

G

garrire (6)	chatter
genus, gener–, n. [1]	race, kind, birth
gerere, gestum [5]	carry, wage
germen, germin– (4)	sprout
gladius (3)	sword
globus (3)	*globe*
gradi, gressum [7]	step, walk [–gred–]
gradus, gradu– (1)	step
granum [3]	grain
gratia [1]	favor, thanks
gratus [1]	grateful, thankful
gravis [3]	heavy, serious
grex, greg– (2)	flock

H

habēre, habitum [7]	have, hold
haerēre, haesum/haesitum [5]	cling, stick
hamus (3)	hook

158

herba (4)	young plant, grass, *herb*
heres, hered- [3]	heir
hibernus (2)	wintry, winter
homo, homin- (3)	human being
horrēre [6]	shudder, stand stiff
hospes, hospit- (1)	host
hostis, host(i) [3]	enemy
humanus [3]	*human*
humēre (6)	be moist
humilis [1]	lowly, on the ground
humus [3]	the ground, soil

I

ignis, ign(i)- [2]	fire
imitari, imitatum [7]	copy
immunis	tax-exempt
index, indic-, m. (1)	forefinger, pointer
insidiae	ambush, trap
insula (4)	island
ire, itum [4]	go
iter, itiner-	journey
iterum (5)	again

J

jejunus (1)	hungry, fasting, insubstantial
jacere, jactum {-io} [4]	throw [-ject-]
jacēre [no ppp.] [4][6]	lie
jocus (1) [3]	jest
judex, judic-	judge
jungere, junctum [7]	join
jus, jur-	right, law

L

labi, lapsum [7]	slip
labor, labor-, m. [1]	work
lacrima	a tear
lassus	tired
latēre (6)	lie hidden
latum [see *ferre*]	carried
latus, later- [2] [3]	side
latus [adj.] [3]	wide
legere, lectum [5]	gather, choose, read
levis [3]	light [not heavy or serious]
lex, leg- [2]	law
liber, liber- (1)	free
liber, libr- [3]	book
libra (2)	balance
limen, limin- (5)	threshhold
linere, litum (6)	smear

```
linquere, -lictum (6)      leave
liquēre [6]                be fluid
littera [1]                letter
livēre (6)                 be black and blue
locus [1]                  place
longus [3]                 long
loqui, locutum [6]         speak
lucēre [6]                 shine, be light
ludere, lusum [5]          play
lumen, lumin- (5)          light
luna (2)                   moon
lupus                      wolf
lympha                     water
```

M

```
magnus [3]                     big, great
major, majus [majes-] [3]   greater, bigger, older
malus [3]                      bad
manēre, mansum [6]             remain
manus, manu- [2]               hand
mare, mar- [2]                 sea
mater, matr(i)- [2]            mother
maximus [3]                    biggest, greatest
medius [adj.] (1)              middle, in the middle
melior [see bonus]             better
memor (6)                      mindful
mens, ment-                    mind
mensa (1)                      table
metus (3)                      fear
migrare, migratum [6]          move, change one's abode
miles, milit- [2]              soldier
mille, mill(i)-                thousand
minimus [3]                    smallest, least
minor, minus [mines-] [3]   smaller, younger, less
mirari, miratum (6)            wonder at
miscēre, mixtum (6)            mix, mingle
miser [adj.] (1) [3]           wretched
mittere, missum [4]            send, let go
modus [1]                      manner
moles, mole- [3]               heap, mass
monēre, monitum (6) [7]     warn, advise
mons, mont-                    mountain
mordēre, morsum [6]            bite
mors, mort- [2]                death
mortuus [2]                    dead body
mos, mor- [2]                  custom, manner, mood   [pl. mores]
movēre, motum [7]              move
multus (2)                     many
mundus (2)                     world
murus [2]                      wall
mus, mur- [3]                  mouse
```

N

nasci, natum [6]	be born
navis, nav- [2]	ship
necesse [2]	unavoidable
nepos, nepot- (1)	grandson, *nephew*
nervus [2]	tendon
nihil (5)	nothing
nomen, nomin- [2]	name
nonus (2)	ninth
novem (2)	nine
novus (5)	new
nox, noct- [2]	night
numerus [2]	number
nuntius (5)	message, messenger
nutrire, nutritum [6]	*nourish*
nux, nuc- [3]	nut

O

oculus [2]	eye
octo (2)	eight
odium [2]	hatred
omnis, omni- (2)	all
onus, oner-, n. [1]	burden
ops, op-	means, resources
optare, optatum (6)	wish
optimus [see *bonus*]	best
opus, oper-, n. [1]	work
ordo, ordin- [2]	rank, row
oriri, ortum [6]	arise
os, or- (4)	mouth
os, oss- [2]	bone
otium	leisure

P

paene	almost
paenitēre [6]	repent
pagus	village
panis	bread
par [1]	equal
parare, paratum [4]	get, get ready
parcus	sparing
pars, part- [3]	part
pater, patr(i)- [2]	father
pati, passum	suffer
pauci [pl. adj.] [3]	few
pax, pac- [1]	peace
pecunia	money
pejor (3)	worse
pellere, pulsum [4]	push
pendere, pensum [5]	hang, weigh

pes, ped- [2]	foot
pessimus (3)	worst
pestis, pest(i)-	plague
petere, petitum [5]	aim at, seek
pingere, pictum [7]	prick, paint
pinna (1)	feather
pius [3]	devoted to duty
placēre, placitum [6]	please, be agreeable
plectere, plexum	weave
plenus [1]	full
ponere, positum [5]	put, place
pontifex, pontific- (3)	high priest
populus [1]	a people
portare, portatum (4) [5]	carry
posse [pot-] [6]	be able
posterus [3]	coming after
potens, potent- (1)	powerful, being able
praeda (1)	booty, *prey*
prehendere, prehensum [5]	seize
premere, pressum [4]	squeeze
pretium (5)	price
prex, prec- (5)	prayer
primus [1]	first
prodigium (1)	portent, monster
proles	offspring
proprius [3]	one's own
proximus (5)	nearest
puer, puer- (1)	boy, child
pulcher, pulchr- (1) [3]	beautiful, handsome
pugnare, pugnatum	fight
pungere, punctum [7]	prick, sting
putāre, putatum	think, consider

Q

quaerere, quaesitum [5]	seek, ask [-quir-, -quisit-]
qualis [3]	of what kind
quantus [3]	how much
quartus (2)	fourth
quattuor, quadri-, quadru-	four
queri (6)	complain
quintus (2)	fifth
quinque (2)	five
quis, quid	who, what
quotus	how many

R

radius, radi- [2]	ray
radix, radic- [2]	root
ramus	branch
rancēre (6)	stink
rapere, raptum [6]	snatch

162

ratio, ration- [2]	*reason*, reckoning
regere, rectum [6]	guide, direct, rule
rēri, ratum [7]	think
rete (3)	net
rex, reg- [2]	king
rigere (6)	be stiff
rodere, rosum (4)	gnaw
rogare, rogatum (4) [5]	ask
rota [1]	wheel
ruga (5)	wrinkle
rumpere, ruptum [4]	burst, break
rus, rur- [2]	the country

S

saeculum [2]	age, the times
salire, saltum [6]	leap, jump [-sil-]
salus, salut- [2]	health, safety
sanctus [1]	holy
sanguis, sanguin- [2]	blood
sanus [3]	sound, healthy
sapiens, sapient- (3)	wise
satis [3]	enough
scandere [5]	climb [-scend-, -scensum]
scire [6]	know
scribere, scriptum [4]	write
scrupus (3)	stone
secare, sectum [5]	cut
secundus (2)	second
sedēre, sessum [6]	sit
semi (2)	one half
senex, sen- [3]	old [man]
sentire, sensum [4]	feel
septem, sept- (2)	seven
sequi, secutum [6]	follow
series (1)	row
servare, servatum [5]	save
servus [3]	slave
sesqui- (2)	one half more
sex (2)	six
signum	mark
similis [1]	like
sinus, sinu- (5)	wave, fold
sistere, statum [5]	set, stand [cf. *stare*]
sobrius	moderate
socius [3]	comrade, ally, companion
sol, sol- [2]	sun
solēre, solitum [6]	become accustomed
solvere, solutum [4]	loosen
somnus [2]	sleep
soror (4)	sister
specere, spectum [6]	look at
species [1]	sight, appearance
spirare, spiratum	breathe

sponte	of one's own accord
squalēre (6)	be stiff, be clotted
stare, statum (4) [5]	stand
sternere, stratum	spread
stimulus (4)	goad
stinguere, stinctum [7]	quench
stringere, strictum	draw tight
struere, structum [7]	pile up, build
studēre [6]	be diligent, be eager, study
studium [1]	eagerness, zeal
stupēre (6)	be stunned
sumere, sumptum [5]	take up

T

tabula (4)	plank, *table*
tangere, tactum [6]	touch [-ting-]
tegere, tectum [7]	cover
templum	sanctuary
tempus, tempor- [2]	time
tendere, tentum, tensum (4) [5]	stretch, aim at
tenēre, tentum [4]	hold, keep [-tin-; -tain]
tenuis	thin
terminus [1]	boundary, end
terere, tritum	rub away
terra [1]	earth, land
terrēre [6]	frighten
testis [3]	witness
texere, textum [7]	weave, build
timēre [6]	fear
tingere, tinctum [7]	dip
tondēre, tonsum [7]	shear, clip, shave
torpēre (6)	be numb
torquēre [tor-], tortum [7]	twist
trahere, tractum [5]	drag, draw
tremere [6]	quake, *tremble*
tres, tri- (2)	three
tumēre (6)	be swollen
turba	riot, uproar

U

ultimus	last
unus (2) [3]	one
urbs, urb- [2]	city
uti, usum [5]	*use*

V

vacuus [1]	empty
vadere, vasum [5]	go, make one's way
valēre [6]	be well

varius [3]	speckled, changing
vehere, vectum [6]	convey
vellere, vulsum [7]	pluck, pull
vendere, venditum [4]	sell
venire, ventum [4]	come
venter, ventr- (3)	stomach, belly
venum [see vendere]	sale
ver	spring
verbum [2]	word
vermis (4)	worm
vertere, versum [4]	turn
verus [1]	true
vestigium (5)	trace, footprint
vestis (4)	clothes
vexare, vexatum [7]	shake
via [1]	way, road
vidēre, visum [6]	see
vigēre (6)	thrive
vigilare (6)	be wakeful
vilis (6)	cheap
vincere, victum [5]	win, conquer
vinum [2]	*wine*
vir, vir- [2]	man, male
virus [2]	poison
vis	force, power, strength
vitium [2]	fault
vivere, victum [5]	live
vocare, vocatum [4]	call, use the *vox* [-voke]
volvere, volutum (5)	roll
vorare, voratum [4]	de*vour*, eat
vovere, votum [7]	*vow*, promise
vox, voc- [2]	voice

Numbers in square brackets refer to lesson vocabularies;   numbers
in parentheses refer to lesson examples or exercises.

Glossary of Greek Base Words

A

acou, acu- [13] [akouein]   hear
acousia/acusia, acousis/acusis [11] hearing
adēn [11] [Latin, glans, gland-] gland
aēr [8] air
aesth-, esth- [13] [aisthanesthai] feel, perceive
ag- [13] [agein] lead, bring
agapē [8] love, *agape*
agōn   contest, struggle [cf. protagonist, antagonism]
agora [8] marketplace
agra [11] violent pain
agros [11]   field, land
ainigma   riddle > enigma
aiōn [8] age > eon
aisthanesthai [aisth-/esth-] feel
aithēr   upper air > ether
aitia [etio-]   [9] cause
Akadēmeia [8] Plato's school
akos   remedy [cf. panacea, autacoid]
akros [acro-] [10] topmost
algesia [11]   excessive sensitivity to pain
algia [11] pain
algos [-algia] [9] pain
allos [allo-] [10] other
anathēma [8]   something set up
anemos   [9] wind   [cf. Latin, animus/anima, breath, spirit]
anēr, andr-   [9] man (male)
angelos [8]   messenger
angos [11]   vessel
anthos [11]   blossom, flower
anthrōpos   [9] human being
aphia [11]   touch
archein [9] begin, rule, be first
arch-   first
-archy [9] rule, government
ariston   breakfast [cf. aristology]
aristos [aristo-] [10] best
arithmos [10]   number
arktos   bear; the north [cf. arcturus, arctic, antarctic]
arthrōn [11] [Latin, artus, articulus] joint
askein   exercise [cf. ascetic, asceticism]
aspis, aspid-   shield, asp [cf. aspidistra, aspic]
astēr [8]   star
asthenia [11] loss of strength
atmos   [9] steam, vapor
auchēn   [11] [Latin, cervix, -ic-, collum] neck
autos [auto-] [10] self
auxē [11]   enlargement
axiōma [8]   that which is thought worthy > axiom
axios [axio-] [8] [10] worthy

167

B

ba-, be- [13] [bainein] go, step, walk
baktērion   staff, cane [cf. bacteriology, antibacterial]
ball-, ble-, bol- [13] [ballein] throw
baptein   dip [cf. baptism, anabaptist]
barbaros   foreign, non-Greek [barbaric]
barus [bary-, bari-, baro-] [10] heavy
bathus [bathy-, batho-] [10] deep
-be [11] life, organism
biblion [8] book
bios [8] [9] life
blast [11] embryonic cell
blenna [11]   mucus
blepharon [11] [Latin, cilium]   eyelash, eyelid
botanē   pasture, herb, grass [cf. botany, botanical]
bous   bull, cow, ox [cf. bulimia, bucolic]
brachion [11] [Latin, brachium]   arm
brachus [brachy-] [10] short
bronchos [11] windpipe
brotos   mortal man [cf. ambrosia]
bruein   grow [cf. embryo]
bursa   the hide, pouch, sac [cf. bursitis, purse]

C [K, Ch] [see also under K]

cardia [11] [Latin, cor, cord-]   heart
carpos [11] [Latin, carpus] wrist
cele [11] herniation
centesis [11] surgical puncture
cephale [11] [Latin, caput, capit-]   head
ceros/cerus [11] horn   [cf. corn, Lat.]
chaitē [11]   [Latin, seta]   bristle
chaos   empty space [cf. chaos, chaotic, gas]
charis   grace, favor [cf. Eucharist]
cheilos [11] [Latin, labium, labrum] lip
cheir, chir- [11]   [Latin, manus]   hand
chele [11]   [Latin, unguis]   claw
chemeia [11]   [chemo-] art of alloying metals > chemicals, chemical
    reactions
chili-, chilo-, kilo- [10] thousand
chlōros [11]   green
cholē   gall, bile [cf. choleric, melancholic]
chondros [11]   cartilage
chor- [13] [chōrein] move
chore [13]   indicates a plant distributed by a specific agency
choros   dance [cf. choreography, chorus, choir]
chrōma, chromat- [8]   color
chronos   [9] time
chrusos [11]   gold
chthōn [10] earth
cin-, kin- [13] [kinein] move
clasis [11]   a breaking up, dissolution

168

clastic [11] pertaining to dissolution
cle- [13] [kalein] call
clin- [13] [klinein] bend, make to slope
clysis [11] irrigation, washing
col [11] glue, jelly, gelatin
condulos [11] knuckle
cop-, com- [13] [koptein] cut
cranion [11] skull
creas [11] [Latin, carn, carn-] flesh
crin-, cri- [13] [krinein] separate, judge, decide
crypt-, cryp- [13] [kruptein] hide
cyesis [11] pregnancy
cystis [11] [Latin, vesica] bladder
cytos [11] [Latin, cella] cell

D

dactylos [11] [Latin, digitus] digit [finger or toe]
daimōn [8] spirit, divinity
deiknunai show [cf. paradigm, deictic]
deinos [11] [dino-] terrible
deka-, deca- [10] ten
dēmokratia [8] democracy
dēmos [9] the people
dendron [9] tree
derma, dermat- [11] skin
despotes master of the house, lord [cf. despotic, adespota]
deutero- [10] second
di-, dy-, do- [10] two
diaita [8] way of living, diet
diakonos [8] servant, attendant
dicastes [8] member of the jury, judge, dicast
dicho- [10] in two
didaskein teach [cf. didactic]
didonai [13] give [antidote, anecdote]
dike [10] justice
diplo- [10] double
dipsia [11] thirst
diskos plate [discus, dish, dais]
do- [13] [didonai] give
doc-, dog-, dox- [13] [dokein] seem, think
doulos slave [hierodule]
doxa [13] opinion, praise, reputation
dra- [13] [dran] do, act, perform
drakon [8] serpent
drom- [13] [dramein] run
dunamis [13] power
dyn- [13] [dunasthai] be able, be powerful

E [epsilon, eta, ai]

echein [13] hold, have
ēchō [8] sound, echo

ectasia, ectasis [11] dilation, stretching
ectomy [11] excision
edema [11] swelling
emesis [11] vomiting
eidos form, shape, thing seen [cf. idea, psychedelic]
eikon [8] image, likeness
einai [13] be
eironeia [8] affected ignorance
ekleipsis [8] a leaving out
elaunein [ela-] drive [elastic]
eleemosune [8] mercy, pity > alms cf. eleemosynary
elektron [11] amber
elthein come [proselyte]
-emia, hemia [11] blood condition
enantios opposite [enantiobiosis]
encephalos [11] [Latin, cerebrum] brain
ennea- [10] nine
enteros intestine [dysentery]
epos [10] word
eran love [cf. eros, erotic]
erēmos [11] lonely, desert
ergon [8] work
esthesia [11] sensation, feeling
ethnos [9] nation, people
ethos [8] custom
etumos [etymo-] [10] true
eu good, well
eurus [eury-] [10] wide

G

gala, galakto- [11] milk
gamos [9] marriage, sexual union
gaster [11] [Latin, venter] stomach, belly
gē [geo-] [9] earth
genesis [11] formation, development
genos [9] birth, race, kind
genus [11] cheek [genyplasty]
geustia, geusia, geusis [11] taste
glōssa/glōtta [9] [11] [Latin, lingua] tongue, language
glukus [glyc-] sweet [cf. glycerine]
glyph- [13] [gluphein] carve
gnathos, genys [11] [Latin, maxilla] jaw
gnō- [13] [gignōskein] know
gonia, -gon [10] angle
gonu [11] [Latin, genu] knee
-gony [9] production of
gram [10] line
graph-, gram- [13] [graphein] draw, write
gumnos [gymno-] [10] naked
gunē, gunaik- [9] woman

170

H [rough breathing]

haima, haimat- [hem-/hemat-] [9] [11] [Latin, sanguis]   blood
hairein take, grasp, choose [cf. heresy, heretical]
harmozein fit together [cf. harmony]
hecato- [10] hundred
hēdonē pleasure [cf. hedonist]
hedron [10] plane [seat]
hek-, hex-, sche-, och-, -uch- [13] [echein] have, hold
helios [9] the sun
helix, helico- [11]   spiral
hēmera   day [cf. ephemeral]
hēmi- [10] half
hen-, en- [10] one
hepar, hepat- [11] [Latin, jecur, jecor-] liver
hepta- [10] seven
heteros [hetero-] [10] other, one of two
heuriskein   find   [cf. heuristic, eureka]
hex- [10] six
hienai send, throw [cf. catheter, diesis, enema]
hieros [hiero-] [10] holy
hippos [11]   horse
histanai [13, sta-]   stand
historia [8] inquiry
histos   [9] web, tissue
hodos [12] road   [anode, cathode, method]
holos [holo-] [10] whole
homoios [homeo-, homoio-] [10] like
homos [homo-] [10] one and the same
hoplon [11]   armor
hōra [8] time > hour
horan [13] see [cf. panorama]
horkos oath [cf. exorcist]
hubris [8] violence, excessive arrogance, hubris
hudōr, hydro-   [9] water
hugiēs [11]   healthy
hugros [hygro-] [10] wet, moist
hulē [11]   material as suffix -yl
humnos [8] song, hymn
hupnos [11] sleep
husteros [11]   later, behind
hymēn [11]   [Latin, membrana]   membrane
hypsos   [9] height
hystera womb [cf. hysteria, hysterectomy]

I

i- [13] [ienai] go
-iatrics, -iatry [11] healing, medical art
iatros doctor
ichthus   [9] fish
icos- [10] twenty
idios [idio-] [10] one's own, peculiar
ischion [11] [Latin, femur, -or-; coxa] thigh, hip

isos [iso-] [10] equal
istos [11] tela tissue
-itis [11] inflammation

K [see also under C]

kai [10] and, plus
kaiein [kau-] burn [cf. caustic, holocaust]
kainos [ceno-, caeno-; -cene] [10] new
kakos [caco-] [10] bad, ugly
kalein call [ecclesiastical, paraclete, epiclesis]
kalos [kal-, calo-, calli-] [10] beautiful
kaluptein hide [apocalypse, Calypso]
kanōn rod, ruler, standard [cf. canonical, canon]
karpos [9] fruit
katharos [11] clean, pure
kenos [ken-, ceno-] [10] empty
kephalē [9] head
kerannunai mix [cf. crasis, crater]
keras, -at- [11] [Latin, cornu] horn
kinesia [11] movement
kinein move [cf. telekinesis, cinema]
klan break [cf. iconoclast]
kleptein steal [cf. kleptomania, biblioklept]
klēros lot, legacy [cleric, clerk]
koinos [ceno-, coeno-] [10] common
kolla [10] [11] glue
kōma, -at- deep sleep [cf. comatose]
kosmos [8] order, universe, adornment
kreas [10] flesh, meat
krinein judge, separate [endocrine, critic, criterion, crisis]
kruos [cryo-] [9] frost
kruptein hide [cryptic]
kuklos [8] circle
kuon, kun- [11] dog
kurios swollen, Lord

L

lab-, lep-, lem- [13] [lambanein] take, seize
laos the people [cf. liturgy, laity]
-latry worship of [idolatry]
leg-, lex-, lect-, log- [13] [legein] gather, say
leipein [lip-] leave [cf. eclipse, elliptical]
lepis, -id- [11] [Latin, squama] scale
lepsy [11] seizure
lethe forgetfulness [lethe]
leukos white [cf. leucemia]
lite, lith [11] stone
lithos [9] stone
logos [8] word, reason
lophos [11] [Latin, crista] crest

luein   [13, ly-] loose, break
lukos   [9] wolf
lura [8]   stringed instrument
ly- [13] [luein] loose, break, destroy
lysis [11] destruction, breaking down

M

magos [11]   enchanter, wizard
makros [macro-] [10] long
malacia [11] softening
mania [11] madness
martur   [9] witness
mastos [11] breast
math- [13] [manthanein] learn
mēchanē [11]   contrivance, machine
megaly [11] enlargement
megas, megal- [mega-, megalo-; -megaly] [10] big
meros [10] part
mētēr, metro-   [9] mother
metopon [11] [Latin, frons, front-]   forehead
metron [8] measure
mimos [8] imitator
mikros [micro-] [10] small
misein [9] hate
mitos [11]   thread
mnasthai [mne-] remember [cf. mnemonic, amnesia, Mnemosyne]
monos [mono-] [10] alone, only, single
mōros [10] fool
morphē   [9] shape, form
Mousa Muse [Muse, museum, music]
muein   close the eyes, shut [mystical, mystery]
murios [myrio-] [10] countless, 10, 000
muthos   [9] speech, story
mys, myo- [11]   muscle
myxa [11]   mucus, slime

N

narkē   numbness [cf. narcolepsy, narcotic]
naus   [9] ship   -naut, sailor
nekros   [9] corpse
nem-, nom- [13] [nemein, cf. nomos] assign, allot
neos [neo-] [10] new
nephos   [9] cloud
nephros [11]   [Latin, renes]   kidney
neuron [11] sinew, nerve [neuralgia, neurotic]
nomos law
nous   mind [noetic]
nux, nukt- night [nyctophobia]

173

O [omicron, omega]

ochlos   crowd, mob   [ochlocracy]
octo- [10] eight
ōdē   song   [cf. ode, epode, palinode, parody]
odia, osmia [11]   smell
odous, odont- [10] [11]   [Latin, dens, dent-]   tooth
odynia [11]   pain
oikos [eco-]   [9]   house, environment
oligos [oligo-] [10] few
-oma [11]   tumor
omma [11]   [Latin, oculus]   eye
omos [11]   [Latin, scapula]   shoulder
onoma [9] name [onomatopoeia, -onym]
oncus [11]   tumor
ont-, -ous- [13]   [einai]   be [root, -es]
ōon [11]   [Latin, ovum]   egg
ophrys [11]   [Latin, supercilium]   eyebrow
ophthalmos [11]   eye
opis, opsis, opsy [11]   vision
ōps, opsis [11]   [Latin, facies]   face
orexia, orexis [11]   appetite
ornis, ornitho-   [9] bird
oros   [9] mountain
orrhagia [11]   rapid discharge
orrhaphy [11]   suture
orrhea [11]   flow, discharge
orrhexis [11]   rupture
orthos [ortho-] [10] straight
-osis [11]   abnormal condition
osphresia, osphresis [11]   smell
osteon [9] [11]   [Latin, os, oss-]   bone
ostomy [11]   formation of a new opening
ostrakon   shell, potsherd   [ostracism]
otomy [11]   incision
oura [11]   [Latin, cauda]   tail
ous, -ot- [11] [Latin, auris]   ear
oxus [oxy-] [10] sharp

P [P, Ph, Ps]

pais, paid- [ped-]   [9] child
palaios [paleo-, palaeo-] [10] old
palin   again   [palinode]
papuros a plant used for making paper [cf. papyrology, paper]
pareia [11] [Latin, bucca]   cheek
pas, pant- [pan-, panto-] [10] all
patēr, patro-   [9] father
pathos   [9] suffering, experience
-pathy [11]   disease, illness
pau-, -pose [13] (with meaning influenced by Latin ponere)   [pauein]
     stop, cease
pedon   soil, ground, plain [pedology]
peira   attempt [pirate, empiricism]

174

```
pelagos [11]    sea
pempein [13]    send  [cf. pomp]
penia  [11]  deficiency
pente- [10] five
pepsia  [11]  digestion
petra   [9] rock
pexy [11]  fixation
pha-, phe-  [13]  [phanai]  say, speak
     pheme  [13] a saying
phag- [13]  [phagein]   eat
phage [13]   one who/that which eats
phagia, phagy [11]  eating, swallowing
phagous [13]   eating
phagy [13]   the habit or tendency to eat
phain-, phen-, phan- [13]  [phainein]  show, cause to appear; appear
pharynx, laimos [11]  [Latin, gula, guttur]   throat
pher-, phor- [13]  [pherein]  bear, carry
philia, phily [11]  love, affinity for
philos [8]  beloved, dear, loving
phleps, phleb- [11] [Latin, vena]   vein
phobia [11]  abnormal or morbid fear
phōnē [8]  voice
phoria [11]  feeling, bearing
phōs, photo- [8] [9] light
phrēn [11]   [sometimes fren-]  midriff, diaphragm, mind
phulē [11]   tribe
phullon [11]   leaf
phy- [13]  [phuein]  make to grow; grow, be by nature
phyma [11]  swelling
planasthai  wander  [cf. planet]
plasia [11]  formation, development
plasty [11]  surgical repair, plastic surgery
platus [platy-] [10] wide, broad
plegia [11]  stroke, paralysis
pleion [plio-, pleo-] [10] more, greater
pleistos [pleisto-] [10] most, greatest
pleura,  [11] [Latin, costa]   rib
ploutus   [9] wealth
pneumon [11]   [Latin, pulmo, pulmon-]   lung
poie-, poe- [13]  [poiein]  make, do
poiesis [11]  formation, generation
pol- [13]  [polein]  sell
polemos [11]   war
polis   [9] city, city-state
polus [poly-] [10] much, many
poly- [10]  many
pompe [8]  a sending > a solemn procession
potamos [11]   river
pous, pod- [9] [11]   [Latin, pes, ped-]   foot
prag-, prak-, prac- [13]  [prattein]  do
presbus  old  [cf. presbyter]
proctos [11]   anus     anus
proselutos [8]  one who comes to a place, proselyte
prōtos [proto-] [10] first
psallein  play the lyre  [cf. psalter, psalm]
```

175

pseudes [pseudo-] [10] false
psilos   bare, plain [cf. epsilon, upsilon]
psychē   [9] soul, breath, life
pterna [11] [Latin, talus, calx]   heel
pteron [11] [Latin, ala]   wing
pteron, ptilon [11] [Latin, penna, pinna, pluma] feather
ptosis [11] prolapse, sagging
pur   [9] fire
puxos [8] boxwood, box, pyx

R [Rh]

rhaptein [11] sew [cf rhapsode, -rhaphy]
rhegnunai [rhag-] break [cf. hemorrhage]
rhe(u)-, rhy-, rho- [13] [rhein] flow
rhetor [11]   orator
rhis, rhin- [11] [Latin, nares, nasus] nose
rhiza   [9] root
rhodon [11]   rose
rhynchos [11]   [Latin, rostrum]   beak,

S

sarx, sark- [10] flesh
sauros [11]   lizard
schisis [11] splitting
schiz-, schis- [13] [schizein] split
schole [8] leisure > school
sclerosis [11] hardening
scop-, skop-, scep-, skep- [13] [scopein] examine, look at
sema, semat- [11]   sign, signal
sepsis [11]   infection
sitos   bread, food [cf. parasite]
skelos [10] [11]   crus, crur- leg
skēnē [8] tent
skia   [9] shadow
skleros [11]   hard
sōma, somato-   [9] [11] [Latin, corpus]   body
sophos [sopho-; -sophy] [10] wise, clever
sophos [8] wise
spasm [11]   twitching
sperma, spermat- [11] [Latin, semen, -in-]   sperm
sphaira [8] a ball, sphere
sphyron [11] [Latin, tarsus] ankle
sta-, ste- [13] [histanai] stand
stalassein drip [cf. stalagmite, stalactite]
stasis [11] controlling, checking, stopping
stat [11] device to check/stop
stear [11] fat
stellein send [cf. apostle, epistle]
stenos [steno-] [10] narrow
stenosis [11] stricture
stephanos [11]   [Latin, corona]   crown

stereos [stereo-] [10] solid, firm
sternon [11] [Latin, pectus, -or-; sternum, mamma]   breast
stethos [9] [11]   chest
sthenos   strength [cf. asthenia]
stichos [9] line, verse
stoa   porch [cf. stoic]
stol-, stal-, stl- [13] [stellein]   send, make ready
stoma, -at- [11] [Latin, os, or-]   mouth
stratos   army [cf. strategic]
strephein [stroph-, strept-]   turn, twist [cf. catastrophe]
stulos   column [cf. peristyle]
sukophantes [8]   informer, flatterer

T [T, Th]

tak-, tac-, tax- [13] [tattein]   arrange, assign, assess
taphos [9] [10]   tomb
technē [9] art, skill
teinein   stretch [cf. tone, hypotenuse]
tektōn [-tect]   [9] carpenter, builder
tēle [tele-] [10] far away
telos [teleo-]   [9] end
temnein   cut [cf. -tomy]
ten-, ta-, ton- [13] [teinein]   stretch out, strain
tetra- [10] four
thanatos   death [cf. thanatopsis, euthanasia]
the- [13] [tithenai]   put, place
theatron [8]   place for viewing
thema [8]   something set, placed
theos [8] [9] god
therapeia [9] treatment
therapon/theraps [9] attendant
therapy [11]   treatment
thermos [thermo-] [10] warm, hot
thēsauros   treasure [cf. thesaurus]
thorax [11]   thorax
thrix, trich- [11] [Latin, capillus, crinis, pilus]   hair
thronos [8]   armchair
thumos [8]   an aromatic herb, thyme
thumos   spirit [thymus]
tme-, tom- [13] [temnein]   cut
tokos [9] birth
tome [11]   instrument to cut
-tomy   cutting
tonos [10] tone, accent
topos [9] place
toxon [11]   bow and arrows > arrow poison > poison
tracheia, bronchos [11]   windpipe
trachus [trach-, trachy] [10] rugged, harsh
tri- [10] three
tripsy [11]   surgical crushing
trop(h)- [13] [trepein]   turn
troph- [13] [trephein]   feed, nourish
trophy [11]   development

tupos [8] mark
turannos [8] king > tyrant

uria [11] condition of urine

xenos   [9] foreigner, stranger
xēros [xero-] [10] dry
xulon   [9] wood

zēlos   eagerness [cf. zeal, zealot, jealousy]
zōnē   belt, girdle [cf. Evzone, zone]
zōon   [9] animal, living thing
zumē [11]   yeast

Greek suffixes will be found in chapter eleven.

Greek prefixes will be found in chapter twelve.

Numbers in square brackets [] refer to lesson vocabularies or
exercises. Some Greek bases not found in the lessons have been
added with examples of words using them.

                         To telos